[signatures]

Shadow Season

by Sigman Shapiro

Illustrated by Brenda Erickson

© Copyright 2014 by Sigman Shapiro

© 2014 Illustrations by Brenda Erickson

All rights reserved.
No part of this book may be reproduced in any form or by any electronic or mechanical means, including information storage and retrieval systems, without permission in writing from the author, except by a reviewer, who may quote brief passages in a review.

For information, contact sanjak65024@mypacks.net

ISBN 978-1-312-69367-8

Dedication

This book is dedicated to Debra for her patience and unwavering faith; and to a small, wise Rabbit who came to me in the long nights and told me what to write.

- Sigman Shapiro

Acknowledgements

Thank you to Brenda for her steadfast collaboration, her creative and talented eye, and for loving these characters who mean so much to me.

Thank you to Pete, Lia and Mike who gave me their time and their wise council

- Sigman Shapiro

The illustrator wishes to thank the author for the trust of his characters to her paper and pen.

She also wishes to thank her family for their support and critique of her representations throughout the process, particularly her daughter, Kristen and her nephew Tom.

Last but not least, she graciously acknowledges her Muse that guides her in all creative endeavors.

- Brenda Erickson

The Only Story

*The shadow with the sad eyes
is no stranger*

*Deep inside our DNA
familiar as a heart beat*

*Ignored for years and, yet,
within us from the start*

*Speaking through our choices
flavoring our mourning*

*The silent presence in our dreams
the subtext of our lives*

*A knowing that transcends
the way we think we know*

*The shadow's story is the only story
the one we cannot change*

*no matter what we do
or why we think we do it*

Sigman Shapiro

1

It was spring and Rabbit was in a beautiful place; the most beautiful place she had ever been. It was a huge meadow and she was sitting in the middle of it. She could see other young rabbits here and there hopping and playing in the sunshine. All around her were lush, green, succulent grasses. Her nose was filled with the sweet scents of the season and a gentle breeze was whispering in her ears. She could not remember a time when she had ever been this happy.

But, something seemed wrong. It was something about the wind. It seemed to have changed from a whisper into a hiss and it was hissing her name over and over again and saying "Wake Up!" Wake Up? What did it mean "Wake up"?

She wanted to yell "Be quiet! Go away!" but she was afraid that her voice would disturb this beautiful place; that shouting was not right here. Then, she shook her head and she was awake.

She found herself in her own cozy sleeping chamber, on a sweet-scented bed of dried grasses. But, if she was awake, why did the wind keep saying her name? She rubbed her sleepy eyes and then she saw the lizard who had poked her head into the room and was hissing

"Rabbit, wake up!"

Rabbit glared at her for a second, angry that she had interrupted her beautiful dream. Then she said "What are you doing in my burrow? Why did you wake me?"

The lizard took half a step back and glanced back up the dark tunnel toward the entrance of the burrow, just to assure herself that she could scoot to safety if the angry rabbit moved toward her. Then she turned back toward Rabbit and delivered the message. "Tortoise told me to come here and tell you he wants to see you now." With that, she bobbed her head up and down twice in a very lizardy way and then scurried back up the tunnel and out into the clearing.

Rabbit stood up slowly from her sweet-scented bed of dried grasses. She stretched and yawned then she wrinkled her brow. "Strange", she thought, "Tortoise never wants to see me before breakfast. What could be so urgent?"

Tortoise was a Spirit Healer and the oldest, wisest creature in this part of the scrubland. He had been her teacher for a whole year now, ever since her first summer.

Most young rabbits spent their first year frisking and playing and flirting their way toward adulthood; she, however, had been different. From the beginning, she had been drawn to the old healer. She would spend hours watching him and listening to him talk to himself, and to the creatures who came to him for help.

Shadow Season

THE RABBIT

Her littermates always knew where to find her. They would hop over to Tortoise's burrow under the pinion and try to draw her into their games. But she would only smile and send them on their way. After a while, they decided she was "different"; they stopped trying to include her and left her to her strange, unrabbit-like behavior.

Tortoise had been skeptical when she first approached him and asked for his help. When she explained that she had felt the calling to be a Healer since she was a small bunny in her mother's burrow, he told her to go play with the other rabbits and leave him alone. But she had persisted, until he agreed to test her and see if she was truly born to the calling. She had done her best to complete every task he gave her and, after a while, he agreed to help her on her journey.

Now, many months later, everyone knew that she was his chosen student and they treated her with a kind of respect and a bit of fear. She wasn't sure she liked that part of things. Rabbits are gregarious by nature and she was no exception. She loved having the other rabbits near her and was sad when she realized that her life choice meant she would always be a little bit alone, even when she was surrounded by her friends.

But, this morning there was no time to think about those things. Tortoise had called for her and that meant she must go to him immediately. Of course, that did not mean she was willing to forgo a few basic essentials. She had to groom her fur and wash her face before she was willing to leave her burrow and be seen in public; and then there was the matter of breakfast.

Half an hour later, Rabbit was sitting in the shade of the pinion tree doing her best to be very quiet and wait for Tortoise to speak. They were an unlikely pair; Rabbit, with her neatly groomed fur; Tortoise, with his heavy, hard shell. She was all graceful, barely bridled, youthful energy. He was lumbering, patient, calm and old, very, very old.

He had a tendency for long pauses and, when he did speak, he would ramble and mumble to himself. Though she had gotten used to this during the months of her training, sometimes it was still almost too much for her to bear. Today was no exception; he talked and talked in his deep slow voice, half to himself, half to her and never seemed to come to the point.

At first she sat quietly, then she began to fidget a bit, finally, when she was about to say "Please tell me why you called for me" as respectfully as she could, he looked at her and said "You have done very well. I have been very pleased with your progress; in fact, I have taken you as far as I can on my own. Now it is time for things to change."

Her heart raced as she heard him say that "others" would come to her and tell her what she must do. When she pressed him to explain, he told her that every healer had to find their path by going on a quest. He said that meant that she must go off by herself to an unfamiliar place and remain in isolation until the "others" contacted her.

There was that word again. She wanted to ask him who these "others" were, how she would know when they contacted her, how was she supposed to act, how would they know where to find her if she was not at home, and a thousand more questions. Instead, she held herself in check and listened to his words carefully.

He explained how to find a secret spot among the rocks, high up on the mesa. There was a bit of clean water there and a few edible plants nearby. He told her that she must not speak to anyone after she left him today and that she should listen to her dreams. He reminded her to use what he had taught her; then he sent her off on her own. The last thing she heard him say as she hopped away was "do not return until you know".

Rabbit headed for her burrow in a kind of daze. The morning had started out so differently, with sweet dreams and soft spring air. Now she was headed for a strange place; as far as she knew, a place no rabbit had ever been. She was going there on a mission, but she did not know what it was, or what she was supposed to do about it. All she knew was she had been told to go far from her safe little home and to wait for some kind of sign to come to her.

She was frightened, but also, strangely excited. She wasn't sure what would happen, but she was sure that Tortoise would not ask this of her unless he believed she could do it. She stopped for a second, and caught her breath. She calmed her racing heart like he had taught her to do; then she turned away from her burrow. There was nothing there she needed. Instead she set her jaw and headed off toward the mesa looming on the horizon.

Sigman Shapiro

2

Coyote was on the hunt. He was crouched down, almost invisible, in the bushes on the edge of a small opening in the brush. He was concentrating intently on the middle of the clearing. He had spotted his quarry and was waiting for the right moment to spring forward and make the kill.

At times like these, Coyote pictured himself as a fierce hunter of the plains; ready to do battle to the death with his powerful prey. Coyote's "prey" in this case was a small, shiny black beetle that was going about its business in the clearing, unaware that implacable Death was watching and waiting in the bushes.

Finally, he grew tired of waiting; he could feel himself losing focus. He realized that he needed to make his move now, so, he tensed his muscles, and with all his might he leaped toward the hapless beetle. He smiled in mid flight; his aim was perfect; he would be on the prey before it knew what was happening. Unfortunately, Coyote's old eyes were not a good as they used to be. In mid leap he slammed his chest into a hard, dry branch that arched up among the bushes. The impact knocked all the wind out of him and sent him sprawling, legs splayed, three feet to the right of his target.

The beetle gave him an indignant look, and immediately opened its wings and buzzed off into the dense brush. Coyote had missed another easy kill.

He pulled his legs in and rested his muzzle on his front paws. He needed to catch his breath and figure out how he found himself in this situation again. This was not the first time he had missed his prey. It had been happening to him quite often lately. Yesterday he had missed lunching on a kangaroo rat when his hip had stiffened and he stumbled as he pounced. The commotion had startled the creature and the slight delay in his attack had given it time to escape before he could grab it.

Was he starting to lose his edge? Was it him the small creatures were laughing at? He could hear their snickers in the brush as he patrolled his hunting grounds. Normally they were as silent as possible; knowing his big ears would zone in on them if they even breathed hard. But lately everywhere he went he heard the sound of rude, high-pitched giggles.

He had been hunting this part of the scrubland since he was a youngster fresh from his parent's den. That was many years ago and through all those years the other creatures had always treated him with respect. But something seemed to have changed. If he didn't figure out what it was and fix this situation soon, his life would become intolerable. With this grim thought, he raised himself on his long shaky legs and walked off stiffly through the chaparral toward a small grove of junipers in the distance.

The juniper grove contained a small pool of water fed by a deep, cool spring. The pool lay at the foot of a small rock outcropping and was surrounded by a soft, green carpet of plants. It was his favorite place; the place he went to rest in the shade, to think, and to get some perspective. He certainly needed perspective today.

Usually, when Coyote approached the pool he would stop on the trail and sniff the wind; then, when he was certain there were no intruders, he would trot up to the small pool, crouch down warily and dip his tongue into the water to drink; but today he was hurting. His head was throbbing and his body was stiff. So, he walked right into the clearing without pausing until he was standing with his front paws in the cool mud; then he leaned far out, ready to plunge his muzzle into the soothing water. As his dim eyes looked down, he gave a startled yelp and jumped straight back, cowering and trembling on the bank.

He had just seen his father's ghost staring up at him out of the water! He was sure it was his father, even though the old coyote had been gone for many years now. There was the haggard face, the drooping ears, the dark circles around the sunken eyes and, most telling of all, the white-furred muzzle!

After a while, in spite of his fear, he pulled himself together and resolved to speak to the spirit; to ask what it wanted from him. So, his heart pounding, he leaned out again with his eyes closed, and then gradually opened them. Yes! There was that old, haggard face, but wait! That wasn't his father! That was him!

He groaned and fell back onto the bank in amazement. When had his muzzle turned so white? How could this have happened to him? No wonder he was missing so many meals! The other creatures could easily see his white face in the brush and escape. They were snickering behind his back because they had seen the white fur and had decided he was old.

Well, they were wrong! He was not old! True, he was having a bit of trouble with his eyes lately, and he was out of shape. His reflexes had slowed and his aim was off too; but he was sure, if he cleaned up his life, got more exercise, ate better, slept more, things would go back to normal and the color would return to his fur.

In the meantime, though, he had to do something about his white face. But what could he do? He didn't even know what had caused it. No matter, he told himself, he was a coyote after all! Coyotes are the cleverest creatures in the Scrublands. He was certain he could find a way to fix this situation if he thought hard about it. When he did, the other creatures would remember to give him the respect he was due and he wouldn't miss so many meals.

With that hopeful thought firmly in mind, he lay beside the quiet pool with his muzzle on his paws and began to think.

As he thought, his eyes darted here and there, looking at his surroundings, as though the answer were somewhere nearby; and, sure enough, after a few minutes his eyes came to rest on the edge of the pond and he chuckled to himself.

He rose back up onto his stiff legs and, his whole body a picture of determination, he returned to the edge of the pond. When he came to the water, he sat back on his haunches and tentatively dipped a paw into the sticky adobe mud at the edge. He removed his paw with a small amount of yellowish mud stuck to the bottom and gently dabbed the mud on one side of his muzzle; then he leaned out over the water again to check his reflection. As he stared at his image, he tipped his head from side to side comparing the whitish gray fur of the clean side with the muddy splotch on the other. "Yes!" he said out loud to himself. There was clearly a difference.

Now that he had seen the result, he sat back down and began to apply his disguise with enthusiasm. He dipped first one paw then the other in the wet, sticky mud and applied the goo to his face. From time to time he would stop and check the results in his reflection.

He continued to smear his face with mud until he was satisfied that every trace of white was gone; then, smiling smugly inside (he could no longer smile with his face) he set off towards his hunting grounds to test the results.

He would show those snickering creatures that he was still a fierce coyote in the prime of life; and remind them who was the predator and who was the prey!

3

Rabbit was sitting at the edge of the cliff watching the sunset. She had been alone here on the mesa for days.

Every evening she had watched the sun slowly slide below the horizon and the scrublands turn dark. Every night she had waited for the sky to fill with stars and the air to chill, then she would turn and hop down into the safety of the cozy burrow she had found and settle in to sleep hoping that, at last, she would see a sign; something that would help her know what she must do next.

Every morning she had opened her eyes disappointed that nothing had changed; that this morning was just like the last morning and all the mornings before it.

It seemed like ages since she had left Tortoise in the shade of the pinions and headed up here so far from everything and everyone she knew. She had started out this adventure with more than a touch of fear at so much change, so much unknown. Her fear of the unknown was very strong, but it was more than offset by her hope and her excitement at the prospect of meeting the mysterious "others" that Tortoise had mentioned.

It was that excitement that had kept her going through the journey from her home to this unfamiliar place. It was also excitement that had kept her searching until she found the sheltered clearing with the cool water, sweet, spring grass and cozy burrow that Tortoise had promised her would be here.

Later, when the excitement had faded, it was her hope that had kept her waiting here through all the long, uneventful days and nights till now; but she could feel that hope fading a little more each day. Soon she would have nothing left to sustain her except her stubborn determination to succeed. She shook her head and forced her thoughts to turn away from her frustration; instead, she gazed out across the land spread out far below her and focused on the last glow of sunset and the cool, rich darkness that was racing across the scrublands to meet it.

Every other night, she had waited a bit longer and then headed for the safety of her adopted burrow. The dark hours were a dangerous time for little rabbits. There were many predators that roamed the darkness and they all would be delighted to find such a tasty meal waiting for them. Some of her earliest memories were of her father and mother warning her and her littermates to always be safe in their burrow before the darkness descended. There was, however, one exception to that rule; that was the night of the full moon.

Every full moon the rabbits would come out of their burrows and dance in the silvery light. It was their way of honoring the Great Rabbit Mother; something that they had done for so long that no living rabbit could remember ever hearing of a time when it wasn't so.

It was a joyful time, especially in spring, when males and females leapt and played together; and it was no coincidence that most litters were born exactly four weeks after a full moon.

Tonight was the night of the full moon and, to honor the ancient tradition of her kind, Rabbit was not heading for the safety of the burrow; instead, she was sitting quietly in a pool of deeper darkness, being as still and invisible as possible, watching the horizon, waiting for the moon to rise.

It wasn't long before she saw the edges of the far peaks that rimmed her world outlined in a pale glow. Her heart beat a little faster in anticipation. If she were back in her real home, surrounded by her family and friends, this would be a time of laughter and joy and love. That thought made her smile, but it also made her sad. She missed her familiar world. Her longing for home had grown stronger every day. It was an ache that never left her; and it was gnawing at the last shreds of her hope.

Sitting there in the darkness, she let her thoughts turn inward and she began to ask herself what kind of foolishness she had gotten into. How long was she going to spend her days sitting in isolation waiting for something to happen that was probably never going to happen? What made her think she was a healer?

Maybe she really was just a simple rabbit. Maybe this was all a big mistake.

She had almost decided to give up, to leave first thing in the morning and return to her family and friends, when something made her open her eyes (she hadn't even noticed that they had been closed) and what she saw made her gasp in surprise and wonder.

It was still night, she could see a sky filled with countless stars; but she was not on the edge of the mesa and she was not sitting, discretely in the protective pool of darkness; instead she seemed to be completely exposed bathed in bright moonlight in the center of a level clearing in the middle of a circular canyon. The rough rock walls rose around her on all sides, their bases shrouded by dense forest and there, before her, were three enormous figures.

On the left was a great, black Raven, on the right a tall Coyote, and between them was a Rabbit. Somehow she knew this was the Great Mother of All Rabbits! For a few seconds they looked at her in silence and then the Mother spoke. Her soft, warm voice seemed to come from inside Rabbit's own mind.

"Rabbit, you have come far on your quest. We are pleased with your progress. Now you must pass another, more difficult test. You will need to use all you have learned and all the gifts you were given at birth."

Shadow Season

THE OTHERS

Next the tall Coyote spoke. "There is a coyote who lives on the scrubland near your home. He is approaching the Great Transformation and is not prepared. His spirit is wounded and needs healing. He is in turmoil and in need of guidance."

Then the Raven said, "You must find that coyote, and help him through this difficult time. Do that, and you will truly be the healer you were born to be."

The Rabbit Mother spoke again, "You will know what to do when the time comes. Trust your heart, use your head, and know we are always with you".

With that the scene faded and she found herself back at the edge of the mesa, sitting in the safety of the darkness. As she looked out across the scrublands, for an instant she saw the full moon reflected in a tiny patch of water far below; then it was gone, as though the moon had winked at her.

She sat there for a few minutes thinking about what she had seen. So those were the "Others" that Tortoise had mentioned. She could barely believe this had happened to her. There had been so many questions she had wanted to ask, but she had been unable to speak. She had been so close to giving up, so close to losing faith in herself. Now her hope and excitement had returned, and her determination was even stronger.

She resolved to return home in the morning and begin her search. Somewhere out there on the scrubland was a coyote she must help. How would she know who it was? What if she missed the chance? How could a rabbit help a coyote?

These doubts and a dozen others crowded her mind; pressing on her, holding her back. Then, through it all she heard Tortoise's voice clear and strong, "Never doubt yourself, it is a waste of time. Trust yourself, do what your heart knows you must do, and all will be as it should."

She gave a deep sigh. Suddenly she was very tired. She turned from the edge of the mesa and hopped cautiously back to spend her last night in her temporary home. Tomorrow would be the beginning of her new life.

Sigman Shapiro

4

Coyote blinked, yawned, and stood up slowly from his sleeping spot. His den was a rough, hollowed out space at the foot of a step bank. It was not as cozy or homey as Rabbit's burrow. There were no fragrant herbs, just a few old, cracked bones piled in the corners. He had pushed them aside to make a space to do his morning stretches. Lately when he woke, his body was stiff and achy; but that didn't stop him from feeling very pleased with the world. When his tight old body had loosened up, he spent a few minutes sitting at the entrance to his den and sniffing the cool morning air before trotting off down his usual hunting trail.

Ever since he had started disguising the white fur on his muzzle things had gotten better for him. His confidence was improved, and his hunting had been more successful. It was not really like it had been in his heyday – but it was far better than in the last few months.

That first day had been a revelation for him. He had left the clearing by the pool unsure if his idea would work. He had trotted along familiar trails that ran through the sage and low scrub, nosing into the brushy thickets where he knew he would find the small creatures that were his usual prey.

As he made his rounds, he encountered clusters of them going about their business in the relative protection of the low canopy. He quickly realized there was a pattern to these encounters. He would turn a corner or duck under a limb and startle a group. Their eyes would grow large and for a moment they would be frozen in place, then they would scatter in every direction seeking any cover they could find.

Once he understood how it would play out, he found he could use that moment of wide-eyed terror to snatch a meal before they got their wits about them. He was eating better now than he had in months. He was even starting to look a little heavy around the middle.

He had used his new strategy to reestablish his dominant position in the scrubland, so that, now, there was none of the laughter and whispering that he had been hearing these last months. Clearly his strategy was working. Now that he no longer looked old and gray, they remembered who he was. They respected him again.

In fact, today he was not going out to look for food; he was patrolling his hunting grounds to remind the inhabitants of who was at the top of the food chain. He was pleased that, instead of the snickers and giggles he had heard in the past, the only sounds he heard now when he set out to hunt were the whispered warnings and calls of alarm that spread out in front of him like a wave as he moved through the scrub.

The word of his movements had spread in every direction by the end of the morning's first hour and he knew he would not encounter any prey for a while. He also knew that their memories were short and that, within an hour or two, the brush would be full of activity again.

He decided to go back to the juniper pool to think and rest up until later in the morning. By then his stomach would begin to complain and it would be time to grab some lunch.

Sigman Shapiro

5

When Rabbit returned from her quest, she had expected that everyone would fuss over her and ask her where she had been. She had it all worked out. She could see it in her mind. The other rabbits would all be curious about her absence and would ask her a thousand questions. She, of course, would not say anything. She would be silent, aloof, and mysterious and they would be intrigued and even more curious. She would be the center of attention, a sort of hero. That would make up, in part, for the days she had spent in isolation. But no one had said anything. In fact, they didn't even appear to have noticed she was gone at all.

She had arrived late in the day, tired and bedraggled and had slipped unnoticed down the tunnel into her burrow. It was good to be home, to stretch out on her soft bed of dried grasses and sleep enveloped in familiar scents.

The next morning, after a solid night's sleep and a good grooming, she poked her head out from under the greasewood shrub that hid the entrance to her burrow and looked around. There were the trails through the scrub that she had hopped down all her life. All around her the shrubs were leafed out in fresh green; some

were even showing signs of blooming after sleeping through the harsh Scrublands winter.
She felt an unfamiliar ache in her heart. This was her home, she had always taken it for granted before; but, now that she had been away for days, she realized how beautiful it was and how much she loved it.

After absorbing the scene for a few minutes she had hopped out onto the trail to see if she could "accidentally" meet any of her friends or family. After an hour spent passing by the places they usually could be found she realized her part of the scrublands was almost deserted. "Something's wrong!" she thought. "This place should be full of rabbits. Where are they?"

She decided set out for the pinion grove to see if Tortoise could explain what was going on; but she hadn't gone far before she ran into a cousin who was hurrying down the trail toward his home. To her, it looked almost like he was being chased by something.

"Hi," she said as he raced by. He gasped and leapt for cover; then peeked out at her from under the bushes. He was a sturdy young buck so she was shocked to see him trembling like Death itself was behind him.

It took him a second to recognize her, then he hopped out from under the brush and gave her a proper, though distracted, greeting; all the while looking left and right as though he were expecting some terrible creature to pop out of the bushes at any moment and slaughter them both.

As they sat there nose to nose, she looked at him as if to say "What is going on?" He looked a bit embarrassed and then he laughed nervously and said "Sorry, I thought you were the Monster!"

"What do you mean?" she said, "What Monster?"

He looked surprised and said "Where have you been?"

Now that was just the question she had been waiting to hear! "No where special", she said, her whole manor calculated to convey exactly the opposite meaning.

But, instead of becoming intrigued by her air of mystery and showering her with probing questions he looked around nervously and said, "The Monster Coyote!" in an awe filled whisper. "Everyone is keeping close to their burrows. I'm headed home now. You should do the same." The last bit was said over his shoulder as he rushed away through the scrub.

Rabbit sat by the trail and watched him as he hurried down the path. She was still sitting there staring in confusion and disbelief when the white flash of his tail disappeared around the bend in the trail.

"Monster Coyote? What kind of nonsense was he jabbering?" If she hadn't known him and known that he was a serious, sensible young rabbit, she would have decided he was playing a prank, or had gotten into a patch of Jimson weed; but she did know him and so

she turned pensive and thought, "What could have frightened him so profoundly?
I'd better check in with Tortoise and see what he knows about this." She turned back down the trail and continued to hop toward the Pinion grove.

When she arrived, she found Tortoise in his usual spot, sitting, half buried in the soft soil in the shade of the pinion tree. He did not seem the least bit surprised she was there. In fact, he seemed as though he expected her. He barely gave her a chance to say hello before he looked at her, nodded toward a spot in the shade and said, "So, Rabbit, settle down and tell me everything. I want to know what you saw, what you heard; and, most of all, what you learned."

She hopped over, plopped down near him and began to tell the story of her vigil. He nodded as she spoke about her feelings of isolation and doubt. He became excited when she began to talk about the night of the full moon; and he listened intently, eyes closed, as she explained the vision of the three great spirits.

She was about to describe the events of this morning and ask him about the strange things her cousin had said, but he spoke first.

"Doesn't it seem like too much of a coincidence that your spirit guides charged you to aid a coyote and you have returned to find rumors of a Monster Coyote prowling the Scrublands?"

His question surprised her. She hadn't made the connection but, now that he said it, it seemed obvious. "What do you think I should do?" she asked.

Sigman Shapiro

6

Rabbit was sitting concealed in the brush near the juniper pool. She was waiting for the coyote to return; waiting to see how much truth there was to all the stories she had heard.

In the few days since return from the mesa, she had spoken to several of the animals that lived nearby. Their stories had been wildly different. Some spoke of a magic beast that appeared out of nowhere and snatched small creatures who were never seen again. Some were certain it was some kind of giant bird; others assured her it was a monster lizard. But, when she filtered out the most outrageous stories she found that the most plausible ones all had a common thread.

A horribly disfigured coyote had appeared in the area suddenly. As far as she could tell it was about the time she had left on her quest. The new predator was terrifying. It had killed the old coyote who had patrolled their part of the scrublands for years, moved into the old fellow's den, and was now spreading fear and death wherever it went.

Once she understood the timing of these events she became convinced that this was some part of her quest. She had to find out what sort of "Monster" this was.

She had a sick feeling in her stomach that when this creature had killed off the old coyote it had killed off the object of her trial and so had ensured that she would fail.

Everyone had been shocked this morning when she explained where she was going and what she was going to do. They were sure it would be the end of her. She wasn't so sure they were wrong, but she had to know. She had to find out what was true; and so, here she was hiding near the old coyote's favorite spot waiting to see if his killer had taken over this place as well as his den.

Coyote trotted into the tiny clearing and flopped down in the shade near the pool. He had come here, as he did most days, to rest for a while; maybe even take a short nap.

He yawned and stretched out his paws, then rolled from side to side trying to find the most comfortable spot. For some reason he could not relax. After a bit he got up and moved to another spot a little closer to the water; but that spot was no better.

He stopped to think about what was bothering him and realized that his muzzle had started to itch. The day was hot, the air was even drier than usual and the coating of mud was starting to shrink and irritate his skin. When he was hunting, it was an asset; right now it was an annoyance. So he got up and trotted to the pool to wash off the mud. He would replace it later when he left to hunt for lunch.

Shadow Season

THE COYOTE

He admired his reflection for a few seconds, then plunged his face into the water and splashed and pawed at the fur until it was all clean and white again. Then he sighed with relief and waited for the pool's surface to become calm. He carefully examined his whitened muzzle in the reflecting water; bending and turning to see it from every angle.

He shook his head sadly at the old coyote he saw there. When he turned away and trotted back to his shady spot to doze for a while, his whole demeanor spoke of sadness and defeat.

Rabbit had seen the coyote come trotting down the trail to the pool. At first, his grotesque face had shocked and frightened her. Her heart raced and she felt a powerful urge to turn and run away as fast as she could; but she forced herself to stay where she was and to remain as still as possible. Her resolve was as much about the danger of becoming visible by moving as it was a reflection of her courage.

Gradually her heart stopped racing and she was able to look past her blind fear to take in the scene in the clearing. Once she shifted her focus from survival to the actions of the "Monster Coyote" she realized that, ugly as he was, he was just a coyote; no more a monster than any of the dozens of other predators that patrolled the scrublands.

That thought gave her a kind of comfort and, having more than a normal rabbit's amount of curiosity, she let herself become immersed in watching what he was doing there by the pool. She realized that she had never seen a coyote do anything but hunt before; nor had anyone else she knew. All rabbits were taught from an early age to avoid coyotes at all cost.

As she watched, he tossed and turned and moved from spot to spot. She recognized his actions. They reminded her of the times she had wanted to sleep but could not find just the right spot for comfort. She was surprised to find that she could see something of herself in this ancient enemy.

She had always thought of predators as a kind of "other"; not the "Others" of her vision, but creatures whose whole being was the antithesis of hers and of all the other creatures that constituted their "prey". Now she was seeing herself as having something simple, something fundamental in common with this coyote.

She was intrigued by his strange behavior as he rose and stared into the water. She was even more intrigued when he began scrubbing at his face in the water. And she almost jumped and gave herself away in surprise when he emerged from the water no longer a "monster" but the very familiar old coyote everyone had assumed was dead.

After her initial surprise she became angry. "It was a trick!" she thought. "It was all a typical coyote trick!"

How frightened all those silly creatures had been by a little mud on his face! Her first impulse was to leave immediately and run through the scrublands shouting the news to every creature she met; but something stopped her.

She waited a few seconds longer and watched as he examined his real face carefully in the pool. It became clear to her how deeply sad he was. Something was troubling him. In spite of his success at terrorizing the small creatures of the neighborhood and filling his belly every day, he did not seem happy; not even smug.

She had a sense that the coyote was mourning something; that he had lost something dear to him, something he could never find again. She felt compassion for him, and her compassion awakened a sense of connection with this ancestral enemy. She felt the beginnings of a need to comfort him, to help him get beyond his sadness.

She had found the coyote of her quest.

7

Coyote dozed for a while in the shade as the sun crept higher in the sky. After a while, he was lying in full sun; he had lost the shade. Gradually, the awareness of the heat and intense light beating down on him penetrated his sleep and woke him. At first he was dazed by the bright light and the last shreds of sleep that clung to his brain; then he realized where he was, and how dry his mouth was from lying in the hot sun.

He stretched and yawned and trotted over to the pool to satisfy his thirst. After a long drink, he sat by the bank and began to give his muzzle a "treatment". He dipped up the soft, wet adobe with his paws and coated his face. From time to time he would stop and check the effect in his reflection. He was talking to himself in a low voice as he daubed the mud on. Words like 'old" and "show them" floated softly but firmly from his lips. He was clearly getting agitated by the process of masking his muzzle.

When he had fully cloaked his white fur in mud, he looked into the pool and nodded. He grinned at himself, careful not to disturb the mask drying on his face; then he started off down the trail to begin a serious hunt for lunch.

He hadn't gone more than a few yards when, in a flash, he decided to visit his old nemeses, the prairie dogs. They were his favorite meal, but also incredibly difficult to catch off guard. Perhaps he could startle one of them like he had the other creatures. That might give him the edge he needed to grab a rare and special meal. A coup like that would not only fill his belly in a satisfying way, it would also send a final, definitive signal to all the creatures on the Scrubland that" Mr. Coyote Sir" was back in town!

When she saw that Coyote had dozed off, Rabbit relaxed a bit and settled in to think about her situation. She was trying to understand what she should do to help this creature, and to decide if she was even willing to do it.

"How can they ask me to heal the spirit of this old coyote?" she thought. "I've never been old much less a male or a coyote. I have no idea what he needs."

"Even if I knew what to do, how could I help him? I can't even talk to him! Why would I do that? Why would I help that murderous, foolish, old dog? "

As she mulled these questions over in her mind, the heat made her drowsy and soon she had dropped into a deep sleep. Suddenly she heard the Great Mother saying, "You will know what to do when the time comes. Trust your heart and use your head".

She woke feeling a rush of energy and looked around her, a bit bewildered. There were the juniper trees, there was the pool and there, lying in the bright sun, was the coyote with his white muzzle shining in the light.

When she saw that Coyote was awake and coming to his feet, she checked the wind and verified that it had not shifted, that she was still down-wind; then, she crouched down deeper into the shade and became very still.

She watched Coyote as he drew himself onto his feet and moved to the pool to drink. She watched as he shook the excess drops from his muzzle and settled down by the edge of the pool. She was intrigued to see what he was up to, and she could not help being amazed by what she saw next.

Coyote was smearing his muzzle with mud! Not just any mud, but sticky adobe clay! The first few times he leaned out over the water she was sure he would wash it off; but, no, he not only did not wash it off, he kept on adding more! He patted and rubbed his face with the goo again and again until he had covered his muzzle completely in a thick yellowish crust.

When he stopped, his muzzle had been transformed into a collection of random lumps and knobs. He no longer looked like any normal coyote Rabbit had ever seen; in fact, he no longer looked like anything but the Monster Coyote who had been terrorizing the scrublands for days and who had come to the pool earlier this morning.

When he was done, he admired his image in the water then turned and trotted back down the trail toward the places where the small creatures lived.

Rabbit had never actually watched a predator go about his business. Like all the other small creatures who spent their days in the shadow of the hunt, she avoided all contact with hunters. All through her short life, whenever a hunter had been near and on the prowl, common sense and her basic instincts pushed aside any curiosity she might feel and drove her to find cover. How many times had she cowered, frozen in fear, heart pounding, trying hard not to imagine what was happening, as she waited for the shadow to pass?

Now she was responsible for this predator. If she was going to figure out how to help him, she was going to have to master her fear. So, taking a deep breath, keeping her distance, and staying safely downwind, she followed him as he began to patrol his hunting circuit.

8

The prairie dogs lived in a village in a large clearing on the edge of the scrub. The colony had worked together to clear all the cover around their burrows and for a good distance beyond them. They had sentries posted throughout the community who kept watch for predators and who sounded the alarm at the first sign of danger. One bark from a sentry and every prairie dog would vanish down the nearest hole.

As Coyote moved toward their village his mind was racing. He had hunted them many times before and, except for a few lucky flukes, mostly involving the old and weak, he had never had any real success. If this was going to work he would need a plan.

He knew he would have to leave the cool shade and step out into the blazing sunlight if he was going to catch one. That meant that he would be seen as soon as he left cover. He would have to move fast or else those damn lookouts would spread the alarm and all his potential targets would dive down their holes and escape. Unfortunately, "fast" was not his word these days. For some reason his reflexes seemed to be fading. His mind knew what to do, and it sent the signals, but his muscles seemed to ponder the whole business for a bit before they reacted.

As he drew nearer to the village he became more cautious and moved quietly as he approached the edge of the bushes. The last few feet he crept very slowly, keeping low and looking for a suitable spot to launch his sortie. He was in luck! There was one young lookout standing very close to the bushes and gazing at a hawk approaching the village. If he could move to the edge of the cover behind the lookout without attracting any attention, he could dash out, grab his dinner and be back under cover before the others could sound an alarm.

Even in his old age Coyote was a masterful hunter. He moved like a shadow along the edge of the brush until he was as close to his prey as he could get and still be concealed. He waited for a few seconds to ensure he had not been noticed; then he tensed his leg muscles and leaped more or less toward the unsuspecting prairie dog; landing a few feet behind him.

The prairie dog spun around at the sound and found the Monster Coyote everyone was talking about standing at his back! His eyes took in the lumpy, misshapen face and he froze in fear and confusion. Coyote grinned to himself and prepared to grab the best lunch he had had in days.

Suddenly, some creature flashed between them. The spell was broken. The prairie dog's instincts took over. He let out a loud bark of distress and dove head first into his burrow. Alarm barks echoed all over the village; and, in an instant not one of the inhabitants was in sight. Coyote's delicious lunch was gone; taken away by a rabbit!

Rabbit had been watching Coyote as he patrolled the bushes. She had seen the fear and confusion of the smaller creatures when they caught site of his grotesque face. Each time she saw a mouse or a bird frozen in its tracks by the sight of him, her heart raced and she froze, not wanting to watch, but unable to look away as she waited for the deadly act to unfold; and each time Coyote walked past the easy prey as though they weren't there. Soon Rabbit forgot all about her fear and revulsion. Her curiosity took over; she had to find out what this coyote was doing!

After a while he turned off on the path to the prairie dog village and she followed at a safe distance. When he got near the clearing where the prairie dogs lived he began to act different. Before, he had just walked straight up to the creatures in the brush and ignored them when they panicked and fled. Now she watched him drop low and creep forward. From nose to tail he was every inch the hunter. He was planning on a prairie dog feast!

When she looked around she saw that dozens of small creatures were moving cautiously out of cover to watch what was going to happen. He would have an audience for his kill. Then it dawned on her what he was doing. The prairie dogs were famous as the most effective creatures in the scrublands at avoiding predators. If the coyote grabbed one of them, he would ensure that the legend of his invincibility would grow enormous.

When he began to circle around toward the lone sentinel she knew what she must do. She inched herself forward till she was crouched right at the edge of the brush at the moment the coyote leapt toward the hapless prairie dog. She took a deep breath and launched herself out, sped straight between them and, without looking back she swerved and headed out into the withering heat of the open land.

She hadn't gone far when she felt the Coyote behind her. "Good!" she thought, the first part of her plan had worked; she had lured him away from his prey. She knew she could outrun him for short distances, but over a long course she would tire and his long legs would get the best of her. Somehow she had to keep away from him long enough for the rest of her plan to succeed. It was a dangerous game she was playing, but something told her it would turn out to be OK.

Every little rabbit was taught what to do in situations like this. The rules were well known, drilled into them by their parents. She could hear her father's voice in her mind as she ran for her life "Never run into the open! Always head for the nearest brush where you can cut and dodge and make their long legs into a disadvantage. And, never run into the wind! Even if they can't see you, their noses are better than their eyes. Don't let them get your scent or they will find you no matter how well you hide."

She knew all that, but she was going to break both rules. She felt the hot wind on her cheek and turned her face into the breeze then put on a bit more speed.

She raced across the open land. Coyote was right behind her and he was gaining!

Coyote was furious. He had been cheated of his public victory. He had lost his chance to show that he was not old, that he was still the dominant creature in this part of the scrubland. The rabbit had taken that from him and he was going to get even. Besides, if he couldn't have a prairie dog for lunch, then a rabbit would do just fine!

In spite of his anger, he made sure he ran smart – he didn't try to catch her right away. Instead he stayed close enough behind her that she didn't dare slow down a notch. He knew if she got no rest, soon she would have no energy left to escape him. When that happened, it would all be over in a blink. One bite, a hard shake, and then lunch.

Rabbit did know what she was doing. She wasn't sure she should do it, but it was the only way she could save herself and teach Coyote a lesson. So, she dodged from side to side and ran as hard as she could into the fiery noonday wind.

She could hear Coyote close behind her, his mud-encrusted muzzle now only inches from her tail. Her heart was pounding and her lungs were starting to burn from the hot air. When her legs began to feel heavy she knew it was time to see if her plan had worked.

She turned toward the brush and headed back to the prairie dog village. She knew the scrubland creatures were gathered in the safety of the bushes watching the drama unfold, and she wanted them to see what was about to happen.

When she got to the middle of the village, she spun around and, heart pounding, she confronted Coyote face to face.

Coyote was startled by the suddenness of her unexpected move. He skidded to a stop right in front of her and, not wasting any time, he leaned forward to snap her up in his powerful jaws.

He leaned forward, but that was all. His jaws did not open to grab the tender morsel right there in front of him. Instead he got a strange look in his eyes and began to whine. He could not open his mouth!

Just as Rabbit had predicted, the heat and wind had dried the adobe clay on his muzzle until it became like brick. His jaws were cemented shut! His face was caked in concrete.

Now that he was not focused on the chase he could feel how tight the clay had become as it shrunk and squeezed his muzzle in its grip. He wanted to howl or yip in pain, but all he could do was whine and claw at his muzzle with his paws trying to scrape the mud-mask off his face.

Shadow Season

THE CHASE

Rabbit watched him for a few seconds, and then having caught her breath, she composed herself, to hide how much she was shaking inside. She looked at him and said "silly old dog! You were only fooling yourself. Learn to accept who you are. It is less trouble in the end." Then she turned and forced herself to hop calmly back into the chaparral.

She was greeted by dozens of small, wide-eyed creatures who fussed over her and sang her praises. She had bested Coyote when it seemed he would surely make a meal of her.

She smiled and warned a few young rabbits among the crowd that they must never do what she had done. Then she went off with a group of her littermates and friends to celebrate her victory.

Coyote spent a long time digging at his face with his claws. He also waved his muzzle from side to side, rubbed it on the ground and, finally, he staggered off to a big rock that rose up out of the scrubland and pounded his muzzle on the jagged surface to break the mud away.

It was hours later when, under the cover of darkness a tired, droopy coyote came slinking back to his lair. The mask was gone and his muzzle was white again; except for the places where the dried clay had pulled all the hair out as it fell away.

His face would hurt for a long time, and he would stick to scavenging carrion until the hair grew back in; unwilling to be seen in such a sad state by the creatures who were his prey and from whom he expected respect.

Sigman Shapiro

9

Rabbit woke late the next morning. She was still feeling elated after her great victory over the old coyote. She decided to go visit Tortoise and share her exciting news with him. She headed to his pinion tree right after breakfast. She couldn't wait to see his reaction. On the way she was imagining how proud he would be of her.

She imagined their dialog as she hopped along; his pride in her success, her modest response, his admiration. The thought made her want to run to see him as fast as she could; but she decided it would be best to arrive poised and act matter of fact as she told her tale.

When she arrived she was surprised to find he was wide awake and seemed to be waiting for her. He wasted no time on formalities. "OK", he said, "tell me what happened; from the beginning."

She recounted the events of the last day, trying to sound modest and matter of fact. In spite of her intentions, her feelings of pride and excitement were obvious right from the start and became stronger and more pronounced as she reached the moment of crisis. "And then I raced between them and alerted the Prairie

Dog. He escaped and I drew the coyote out into the sun where I knew his adobe mask would dry and prevent him from making any more creatures into food that day!" She was so caught up in her story she failed to notice that Tortoise did not appear to share her enthusiasm.

Her voice trailed off when she finally noticed his silence. She stopped recounting her great coup and looked at Tortoise. His face was somber and he was staring at her with a stern and disapproving expression. She was shocked! How could he not approve of her actions? She had unmasked the coyote and had prevented him from frightening and killing defenseless creatures with his silly tricks.

There was a moment of uncomfortable silence while Rabbit fidgeted in Tortoise's hard, unblinking stare; then he began to speak. "What made you think that you were supposed to prevent the coyote from capturing his food? The spirits that came to you in your vision did not ask you to protect the other creatures from Coyote; they gave you the task of helping him find his way through a hard time in his spiritual journey. They did not ask you to see to it that he starves to death!"

In spite of herself, Rabbit gasped and hung her head. Tears formed in her eyes as Tortoise went on. "You are supposed to prevent him from fooling himself – not from fooling his prey. Once you asked to become a healer, you put yourself outside the everyday reality of your fellow creatures. You accepted the responsibility to see things as they really are and to act accordingly; for all the creatures in your care. I can not allow you to continue your task with him unless you prove you are able to see beyond the ordinary view of these matters and are ready to rise above the petty considerations of hunter and prey."

Rabbit became more and more confused and resentful as she listened to Tortoise. How could he expect her to sit by and watch that nasty old dog butcher defenseless creatures? How could he expect her to favor that old murderer over smaller, weaker animals? Did he really think she could accept that as her role as a healer?

Tortoise waited for a moment to allow his words to sink in as he watched the storm of doubt, anger, and disappointment cross her face; then he continued. "Hunting is Coyote's lot. He was born to it. He did not choose it. Nor can he change it. He will be a hunter till he dies."

"I want you to go back to your den and carefully consider what I have said. You must stay away from Coyote until you convince me that you understand the true nature of hunter and hunted. Here are three thoughts I want you to ponder. They should help you understand."

"First, we are all part of Life; Life is not part of us."

"Second, Life is constant. It is neither increased by birth, nor decreased by death. It simply changes form"

"Finally, All Life feeds on Life."

"Think about these three ideas carefully and when you feel you understand, return to me and explain them. Then I will decide if you may continue to look after Coyote."

With that, he pulled his head into his shell in a clear signal that their interview was over.

It was a sad, confused, and embarrassed Rabbit who turned and hopped slowly away. She was barely able to hold back her tears. She hoped that she would not meet any other creatures along the way. If she did and they praised her, she wasn't sure she could keep from bursting into sobs.

She was almost home when a delicious smell tickled her nose. The wind carried the message that the red willows were in bloom. Their catkins must have opened during the night. In spite of the turmoil of her emotions, she couldn't help but respond to that scent. It was a favorite treat that was only available for a few days each year.

She decided that she needed to do something nice for herself after the disaster of the morning, so she put Tortoise's instructions on hold, turned away from her burrow, and headed toward the tiny creek where the willows flourished in the damp spring soil.

Sure enough, when she came to the clump of willows, there they were; soft catkins hanging from the branches waiting to be nibbled by hungry rabbits!

Shadow Season

THE RED WILLOW

The bees had found the blossoms already and the air was filled with the sounds of their presence as they moved from catkin to catkin collecting sweet nectar.

She hopped up to a willow bush, her nose wiggling with delight, picked out a particularly fat, tasty looking catkin, closed her eyes, and leaned in to sniff it.

Suddenly everything changed! She was no longer sniffing the willow bloom. In fact, she was no longer a rabbit!

She struggled to hold back her panic and to understand what was happening to her. She could not feel her nose, her ears, her beating heart. Was she dead? Had some predator grabbed her and snapped her neck in that unguarded moment?

Gradually she calmed herself. She became aware that she was not dead. She was alive; but she was not a rabbit, she was a red willow!

She could feel the warm sun bathing her leaves in light; its heat drawing moisture up and out through every leaf. She felt her roots deep in the cool darkness of the moist earth, drawing in the mineral rich water. She felt the moisture flowing up through her body; up and out as though it were gentle music. And she felt her catkins, the bees bumbling through them, the quiet thrill when the pollen was exchanged and the seeds began to form.

She could feel the life flowing through her, and it was beautiful. She was at peace. She was alive.

Then, just as suddenly as it started, it stopped. She was a rabbit again, beating heart, twitching nose, fur, ears, all was back to normal. She was a rabbit again, but she was not the same rabbit. The world was back to normal again, but it was not the same world; would never be the same world again.

That was when Tortoise's words came to her "Life is not in us, we are in Life".

Yes, she saw it clearly now. The same Life that found expression as the red willow also found expression through her as a rabbit. She and the willow were the same. In fact, she and everything around her were the same! The knowing left her breathless. She was frozen in thought there beside the red willow. If a predator had come along she would not have been able to move; just like the red willow was unable to move when she came along to feast on its catkins.

Then she heard Tortoise saying "All Life feeds on Life". Of course! The Life in her fed on the Life in the red willow and, in turn, the Life in Coyote fed on the Life in her. In that instant she knew what Tortoise meant when he said "Life is constant. It is neither increased by birth, nor decreased by death. It simply changes form."

She seemed to wake from a dream, no longer immobile, instead filled with a wonderful energy and excitement. She wasn't sure how he had done it, but she was sure that, Tortoise had arranged for her to receive this enormous gift. She glanced at the willow all decked in its beautiful catkins, then turned and hopped off toward her burrow. She no longer felt resentment; no longer felt the need to fight back tears. Instead, she let the tears flow; but they were not tears of shame and disappointment, they were tears of wonder, ecstasy and joy.

10

Coyote mumbled in his sleep. He was having a wonderful dream. Something delicious was tickling his nose and he was going to go find it. He woke and found that he was no longer curled on his bed. Instead he was sitting up at the doorway with his muzzle pointed out the entrance of his den.

"What is that wonderful smell?" he asked dreamily. He shook his head to wake himself and then he realized what had disturbed his rest. "Female!" he said.

Somewhere up-wind there was a female coyote and she was in a mood to pick a mate. It had been a long time since Coyote had been courting; so long he was not sure he remembered how. Nevertheless, he decided to go looking for her, just to see…… well, just to see.

He headed out in the direction of her scent. As he trotted along he thought about his courting days; it seemed like it was only a short time ago. In his memory it was all excitement and success. He remembered himself as highly attractive; the females couldn't resist his charms.

He was sure he had truly felt wonderful in those days, and he knew he was certainly younger then! There was no feeling to compare with trotting through his hunting grounds with a slim young female by his side. He always felt like the other creatures were watching him with envy; like he was the undisputed master of all his territory.

Even now, as he trotted along, it seemed to him he felt stronger, more focused. He was certain he looked much younger, and that any young female would fawn at the chance to be with a striking, accomplished, experienced coyote like him.

He began to visualize their meeting; to rehearse his part, and to freely imagine her dazzled responses. By the time his nose told him he was near her he had the whole interchange worked out in his head. It was going to be one more in what he remembered as a long string of triumphs.

He broke through the brush suddenly and there she was! She was standing in the middle of a clearing and, to his dim old eyes, she was the most beautiful sight he had seen in many seasons. She turned to look at him and his legs went weak. He was certain he had seen adoration in those beautiful brown eyes.

He was about to walk up and claim his prize when he realized they were not alone. There were two young males in the clearing, and two more were emerging from the brush behind them. At first he was taken back by the presence of so many potential rivals. But, when he looked them over, he decided they were just "pups" and no threat at all. So, he pulled himself back up to his full height and trotted over to the enchanting object of his newly reawakened desires.

Rabbit had been outside Coyote's den when he emerged in his mating trance. The full moon had come and gone twice since she realized she was responsible for the "silly old dog". In all that time she had been careful to arrive near his den early each day to keep an eye on him. He was a late sleeper and so, she usually had plenty of time to clean her whiskers and ears, even to grab a few bites of something green and dewy moist, before he emerged for his daily rounds.

But today was different. She had just hopped into a safe place down-wind of his front door when she noticed his nose poking out into the early morning air. "Now what is that silly old dog up to?" she giggled. She knew coyotes hate being called "dogs"; it was a private joke for her.

He was certainly acting very strange. Not only was he awake far earlier than usual, but he walked out of his den with is nose in the air and a far away look in his eyes. Then, instead of heading out on his usual hunting trails, he began to trot across country in a straight line through the brush. She decided to follow him and see what was so enticing.

As she followed from a safe distance, she could see he was strangely distracted. He ignored the meandering trails that would have made his journey easier, and he walked right past several startled creatures without paying any attention to them. Any one of them would have made a perfect breakfast for the normally hungry beast. But today, it seemed like food was the last thing on his mind.

Finally, they arrived at a clearing in the brush. When she watched him enter the clearing and saw his reaction to the female coyote standing in the center, she understood what was going on. He was in a mating mood!

She shook her head at the idea. How could an old wreck of a coyote like him think he could hope to win a vibrant young female like the one in the clearing? And, even if he did, how could he hold up his end of the bargain and take on the hard work of helping her raise the litter of pups that would be the outcome?

It was clear he was lost in another of his youth-restoring fantasies.

As Coyote approached the female he was certain he saw a look of admiration and submission in her eyes. Once again his dim eyesight had misled him. What she was really feeling was far from submission!

At first, when she saw him she was surprised. "What is such an old fellow doing here?" she thought. In a glance she took in his boney flanks, his gray muzzle and his knobby, shaky legs. She couldn't believe he could have mating in mind.

She stood there confused as he approached her; unsure how to react to his advances. Why was this happening to her? She was a kind young coyote and had been taught to respect her elders. Besides, this old fellow reminded her of her father. But she hadn't invited him to court her and she certainly wasn't interested in him as a mate! She looked at each of the other four suitors as if asking for an answer from one of them.

The suitors were equally confused. They had come fully prepared to compete with their rivals for her favors; but they hadn't counted on this!

Rabbit watched Coyote walk up to the female. She was a female herself, so she could see the awkward position the young coyote was in. She could almost feel her confusion as if it were her own.

She also understood that her reticence would quickly turn to anger if Coyote continued his advances; and then there were the other suitors. They were holding back in confusion for the moment, but, if things progressed, they would likely become violent. The situation was growing very dangerous.

The coyotes were distracted. They hadn't noticed her yet, even though she was clearly up-wind of at least two of them. She knew they were lost in their mating haze and were not likely to go running after a rabbit breakfast as long as that trance held them in its grip.

She needed to act quickly if she was going to defuse things; but what could she do? No sane rabbit would go anywhere near six coyotes! No sane rabbit would even be standing here watching them, much less intervening in their business. Her mind raced through everything she knew about coyotes as she tried to find a way out of this mess.

Every well brought up young rabbit was carefully taught about every aspect of coyote behavior. It was a matter of survival for them. Their elders schooled them in rabbit lore that had been learned through painful experiences and handed down for generations. It was this rabbit wisdom that she turned to now. What had she learned about coyote courtship rituals that might help her?

Then it came to her! Of course!

She began to circle the clearing; staying just out of sight and moving as quietly as she could. She kept one eye on the coyotes as she went. So far no one had decided to take the initiative. She just needed a few more minutes to put her plan into action.

By the time she had reached her destination it was clear the tension would not hold much longer. She had to act fast or her "patient" would be lucky to come away with only his ego torn and bleeding.

She slipped up next to a young male who was standing near the bushes. His gaze was fixed on the female and the old coyote who was approaching her, so he didn't notice the small rabbit by his side. She looked up at him and in her best imitation of a coyote voice she said "Why not do the Mesa Run?" then slipped back into the bushes and made herself as small as possible.

The effect was perfect. The young coyote tilted his head and then spoke to the others as if the idea had just occurred to him. "Yes! Let's run the Mesa Trail!" The young coyotes all turned to look at the one who had spoken.

The Mesa Run was an old coyote courtship ritual. About a mile away across the scrubland was a massive mesa. Its sheer sides rose a couple thousand feet above the plain. There was an ancient coyote trail that zigzagged up its rocky face.

Rival suitors would race up that trail and, when they reached the rock promontory at the top, they would give out their best, strongest howl. In this way they could show that they not only had the stamina to run the grueling trail, but that they still had the strength to give out a powerful howl at the end.

The female would climb the gentler back slope and wait for them at the top of the Mesa. She would watch their performances, looking for the suitor who had the strength to be the best provider for her and her litter of pups. When the race was done, she would choose her mate based on the prowess he demonstrated.

The young males looked at each other and nodded. It was clear they were relieved. There was no way this old fellow could make that run – so they would not be forced to run him off. The young female was also relieved. She would not have to explain or convince her old suitor to go while trying to save his feelings.

Where moments before there had been tension, now the clearing was full of youthful energy. The young suitors were all excitedly discussing the rules and the route to be followed. The object of their desires had moved to join them and was listening and nodding her assent as the plans took shape. They had all turned their backs on Coyote.

$=$

Coyote wasn't sure what had happened. One minute a lovely dream seemed to be within his grasp; the next she was chatting with those four pups and ignoring him. Perhaps this was a test; to see if he was serious about his advances? That must be it! She was playing coy to see if he would follow her and take the initiative.

Well, he certainly was not one to be shy! Not when there was a prize like her to be won. He trotted over to the group, sat down next to her, and tried to look like everything was already settled and they were a couple. She glanced at him out of the corner of her eye, then moved away a few inches to remove any impression they were together.

At first he wasn't sure what they were talking about so excitedly, and then he heard the words "Mesa Run" and his ears perked up. He hadn't thought about that old custom in a very long time.

So that was what they were up to? They were going to show off for her to see who could win her favors. He chuckled to himself. He had won more than a few of these runs in his day. He even knew a secret shortcut. It wasn't strictly fair, and it was terribly steep and tricky going, but he wasn't above a trick or two where mating was concerned.

He listened as they set the time for the run. The males would all meet at the foot of the cliff late in the day. They would start their run just as the sun touched the rim of the western mountains. If all went as it should, they would finish in the dark just as the full moon rose over the scrubland.

Coyote was confident he would be waiting for them with his new mate when they arrived at the top, tired and breathless. It was all he could do to keep from laughing at the thought.

They all headed off in different directions to rest and prepare for the ordeal. Coyote was reluctant to leave the female, but he knew it was only for a short time, and then they would be together, just the two of them.

—

Rabbit watched from her hiding place as the coyotes all gathered and discussed their plans. When they all split up she followed "her" Coyote as he trotted back to his den. He went inside and laid down to rest before the evening's events.

She was glad he wasn't up to any of his usual foolishness right now. That meant she would have time to eat a little and rest before leaving early for the summit. She wanted to get there well before the rest of them so she could find a safe place to hide and watch the climax of the race.

She hopped off to a shady spot she knew, where the ground was damp from a hidden spring and the grass was tall and green. It had been quite a morning! In all the fuss she had not had time for a proper breakfast and her belly was rumbling angrily at her. She settled in to the soft shade to rest and to have something to eat.

A few hours later, when the sun had passed its zenith and the heat of the day was beginning to soften, she shook herself awake from a sweet dream of playing leapfrog with her littermates. She gave her fur a quick grooming and began the long trip to the top of the mesa. She checked in at Coyote's den even though it wasn't really on her way. She could tell by his loud snores that he was still sleeping.

She knew his gift for getting himself into trouble, so she was reluctant to leave him on his own. She shook her head in amazement at the thought. Could she possibly be growing fond of that silly old dog? Nonsense! He was just a nuisance! He would have to get to the starting point without her watchful eye.

She turned her back on the noisy creature and set off toward the high ground.

11

Coyote woke feeling troubled. He had been dreaming about the young female. In his dream he kept approaching her and she would laugh at him, then snarl and snap when he got close to her. Try as he might, he could not mate with her.

The dream frightened him a bit and that made him grumpy and irritable. He trotted out of his den grumbling under his breath and went to the pinion pool to get a drink.

Since the affair of the mud mask Coyote had avoided looking in the pool when he went for water. This time was no different. He approached the pool, then closed his eyes and lapped the water with his long tongue.

When he'd had his fill, he shook the drops from his muzzle and trotted off toward the Mesa. Along the way he passed a group of crows and vultures feasting on a dead armadillo. Normally he would not pass up a chance to sneak in and grab a few mouthfuls for himself; but this was not a normal day.

He was not going to weigh himself down with a belly full of food right before the race. So, he made a mental note of where they were (no harm in checking back after to see if anything was left) and he continued on his way to the clearing that would serve as the starting point for the race.

Three of the young males were already there when he arrived. They were yipping and wrestling and posturing like puppies! The clearing was full of the sound and movement of their antics. Coyote snorted and kept to himself. He was much too dignified to engage in such silly play.

The last young male arrived just as the sun began to approach the rim of the mountains. The suitors all stopped their play and watched the sun's progress. They were poised to race up the trail as soon as it touched the western horizon.

It seemed to take forever, but finally the gap between the fiery ball and the mountains closed and the race was on! The four young suitors raced ahead, each one vying to outrun his rivals. Coyote followed a distance behind. He was not going to waste his energy in such foolishness. He would be at the top and still fresh when they lay panting and exhausted on the trail trying to catch their breath. That was the benefit of wisdom and experience.

The trail was a series of steep switchbacks that traversed the face of the cliff. They were narrow and littered with sharp rocks. The first four switchbacks were long and relatively gentle. After that, each one got shorter and steeper until, near the top, you were climbing over boulders, and it became more like a giant's staircase than a trail.

It had taken Rabbit a while to reach the top. She had taken the gentle trail up the back side of the mesa. It was longer, but it was far less grueling than the trail up the face of the cliff, and she still arrived in plenty of time to settle in before the coyotes came. She even had time to find a few nibbles of sweet, moist green to refresh her along the way.

The mesa was a rough plain dotted with small juniper trees and clumps of scrub. The plain gradually slanted up to end abruptly at a high cliff. It was the face of that cliff that the coyotes would be climbing. Their race would end at a wide open space at the edge of the highest point.

She looked around until she found a safe spot that offered a good view and was down-wind of the finish line. Quest or no quest, she was certainly not going to offer her scent to six hungry coyote noses at the same time!

She settled in and took a short nap as she waited for the show to begin.

The female coyote arrived a while later. She had taken the longer route as well. She looked around and chose a shady spot by the open space to lie down and wait. Once the sun touched the horizon, she moved to the edge of the cliff, where she could gaze down on the trail below and try to watch her suitors' progress.

At first there was no sign of them except the sounds of falling rocks and gravel dislodged as they raced up the trail. Later, she caught glimpses of them between the rocks as they made their way back and forth across the face of the cliff in the gradually dimming light.

As the light faded to twilight and the sounds indicated they were getting closer, she moved back from the edge and waited to see who would be the first to arrive.

By the time Coyote reached the end of the fourth switchback the others were well ahead of him, but he wasn't worried. He stopped and scanned the face of the cliff looking for the entrance to the shortcut. Then he saw it. Yes! It was still there.

What he saw was a narrow, rubble-filled slot between two giant boulders. He squeezed up into the opening and found himself on a steep incline filled with the debris of the decaying cliff-face. He would need to scramble up the loose rock slide for most of his ascent.

He made a great, enthusiastic leap forward and immediately slid back half the distance. He stopped for a second to regain his footing, and then began the long scramble up the shifting rocks.

Shadow Season

THE LOVER

The route was definitely the old shortcut. It was a more direct way to the top, and he did climb faster than the switchbacks would allow, but the effort was monumental. The trail seemed to have gotten steeper, more difficult than he remembered.

Every few minutes he could hear the sounds of rocks falling from above; signs of his rivals' progress. Twice he was showered with rock and gravel dislodged by their feet and had to dodge the larger bits to keep from being injured. His body was hurting and he was growing more weak and tired by the minute.

As he climbed, the trail seemed longer and the obstacles seemed higher, more treacherous. His heart was pounding. He could hear the sound of it drumming in his ears. It was getting harder and harder to catch his breath and his legs felt heavy; like they were made of the same stone as the cliff. He could feel exhaustion beginning to take hold.

More than once he lost his footing and fell a few feet onto the rocks below. Those were terrible moments, when he shook with fear; envisioning himself plunging over the edge and being dashed to pieces far below. When the last of the light faded and he could no longer see the bottom for the deepening shadows, he just pointed his nose up and never looked back. He kept going by telling himself he was going to win; and by envisioning the shock and envy in the faces of his rivals when they arrived to find him in possession of the prize.

Finally he came over the edge of a boulder and found that he was standing near the top of the last switchback. His rivals were nowhere in sight! He had done it! That was when he heard the chorus of long, piercing howls echo from the top of the mesa. Someone had beaten him. Someone had got there first!

Rabbit watched the female as she paced back and forth in the dim light, waiting for her first suitor. The full moon was rising and the clearing was bathed in its pale light when he finally arrived.

He was the largest of the young males. He sauntered into the clearing, trying to look refreshed and confident. He knew he was first. He had passed all the others a while ago and none of them had been able to regain the lead. He eyed the female and then trotted to the edge of the cliff.

He sat down, titled his head toward the sky and let out a long, eerie howl in honor of the moon that shone in the clear, black night.

She continued to watch as, one by one, the other three young males arrived over the next few minutes. Each one stepped to the edge of the cliff and added his voice to the growing chorus singing to the moon.

After a while, the female joined them, nuzzling the strong, young male who had clearly won the race and trotting at his side as they all moved off back down the mesa. There was still no sign of Coyote!

Rabbit was worried. She had initiated this test to show him how foolish it was to compete for the favors of a young mate, one who might well have been one of his own pups. She wanted him to learn the lesson, but she did not want him to be hurt in the process.

She was just about to head down the switchback trail to see if she could find him when he came walking slowly into the clearing. He was panting and limping, and his head and tail were drooping. He seemed exhausted.

He looked around, walked to the edge of the cliff and let out a long, sad, broken howl.

12

Coyote was feeling discouraged. It was about an hour before dawn and he was headed home from another disappointing night of hunting.

He was trotting by the big rock on his way to the waterhole, to get a drink before returning to his den, when he heard someone calling him. He didn't recognize the voice. It sounded harsh, croaking, unlike any creature he knew from the scrublands. He stopped and looked around; sniffing the air to get the scent of the stranger; then he heard the voice say "Up here Coyote. On the rock." He looked up to the top of the big rock and there in the dim light, he saw a huge black bird with its wings spread.

It was a raven! He had never actually seen one before, but he had heard many stories about them, starting when he was a pup in his Mother's den. They were known as the wisest, most magical of all creatures. In the stories that were told on the scrublands, seeing a raven meant something important, something life-changing was going to happen to you.

Coyote sniffed the wind trying to get the creature's scent; but the wind was at his back, the creature was downwind, and the scent eluded him. He squinted at the black silhouette trying to focus his old eyes. Yes! He was certain that this was indeed a raven calling to him! The idea shook him and he sat back on his haunches, with his nose pointed at the rock in awe, unable to answer.

For a moment the raven stared down in silence from its high perch. Its inky feathers were like a pool of deeper darkness against the starless sky; then it began to speak.

"You are sad Coyote. Time is catching up with you and life is growing harder. You feel like there is no hope. But you are wrong. The Great Raven has sent me here to help you. I can give you back your strength, your youth, your life; but you must do exactly as I say."

Coyote sat there transfixed, silent as the Raven explained what he must do.

—

Every hour of every day dozens of creatures, big and small, passed through the clearing at the foot of the rock outcropping on their way to the waterhole for a drink. Today was no different. The sun had barely begun to rise behind the rock when a kangaroo rat came skittering by. He stopped in a pool of deep shadow at the edge of the brush, poked his nose out, sniffed the air and looked around cautiously to be sure it was safe; then he hopped out into the open.

As he turned toward the waterhole, he heard strange croaking noises and looked up at the rock.

Shadow Season

THE RAVEN

At first his eyes were dazzled by the light of the sunrise, then he caught sight of something huge and black haloed with the rosy light of dawn. He stared for a second, transfixed by the image, and then he gasped and turned to race back the way he came. As he hopped down the trail he was repeating one word in his high, excited voice "Raven!"

The news spread quickly through the scrubland community. The sun had barely cleared the horizon and everyone was already talking about the mysterious appearance of the raven. There were many skeptics; the rat was young and he was clearly flustered by what he thought he saw. Besides, what sensible animal could believe a tale about a giant raven spirit enveloped in flames revealing itself to such a creature? Each species felt that members of their clan were much more likely to be chosen for such an important honor.

The jackrabbits in particular were not ones to wait around, and so, within the hour, their leaders met and quickly agreed that one of them would be far more suitable an authority to confirm the presence of the raven to their neighbors. After discussing it for a bit, they decided to chose one member of their clan to go to the clearing and report back what was really happening there. They asked for volunteers and one stepped forward who was known to be brave and level-headed. Everyone agreed he was just the fellow for the job and they sent him on his way with instructions to do a careful assessment and to return as quickly as possible with his report.

The scout left immediately and arrived at the edge of the clearing in a few minutes. Like the kangaroo rat, he too stopped in the cover of the brush before entering the clearing. He lifted his nose and sniffed the air for any strange scents. The morning winds usually blew toward the rock. This morning was no different; he was not able to learn anything that way. He waited for a few moments, trying to decide what to do. Finally he sighed and, his big ears alert for any sound of danger, he stepped out into the clearing and looked around cautiously. As he turned to gaze up at the rock he heard a croaky voice say "Welcome little brother. I have come to help you."

Rabbit had heard the rumors while she was enjoying her breakfast. She was pretty certain it was just one of those silly, groundless flurries that swept through the scrubland communities from time to time; but, to be sure, she decided to check in with Tortoise. If anyone would know what to make of this, he was the one.

She hopped over to the pinion grove and found her mentor dozing and softly snoring in the shade of the pines. For a while she waited quietly and respectfully for him to notice her, but rabbits are notoriously impatient, and she was no exception. After a few minutes she thumped her foot on the ground hard and Tortoise slowly opened his eyes.

"Oh, it's you Rabbit." He said. "I was lost in thought. What can I do for you?"

Rabbit explained about the kangaroo rat's claim that he had seen a raven at the big rock by the waterhole. She expressed her skepticism and asked Tortoise what he thought about it. Was it likely that a raven would appear to them in that way?

Tortoise listened carefully to her and then he surprised her. "I do not like the sound of this." he said. "I will have to make some inquiries before I am certain. In the meantime, please be my eyes and ears. Keep a close watch on things and let me know if any more strange things happen".

He told her he would let her know as soon as he could confirm or dismiss his suspicions. She promised to be vigilant and to keep him informed of events in the surrounding area and hopped off home to plan her next moves.

She was headed for her burrow when she met a jackrabbit racing down the trail. He was trembling with excitement as he told her that his clan had a big announcement to share about the raven and that everyone was invited. He said that he was on his way there and encouraged her to come along. She smiled and thanked him and the two of them hurried to the clearing where the jackrabbits held their meetings.

—

The news spread that the jackrabbits had sent a scout to the rock and that he had returned with a message from the raven. Creatures of all sorts began to converge on the clearing that was the jackrabbits' meeting place. Soon the edges of the clearing were crowded with dozens of creatures of every size and shape; all of them hoping to hear what the raven had said. The jackrabbits were suddenly important, suddenly the center of attention; and they loved it!

The eldest jackrabbit held up his paws, then, when all the creatures were quiet and all their eyes were on him, he pulled himself up to his full height and, in a loud voice, he made the following announcement.

"We jackrabbits have confirmed that there is a raven among us. He has asked us to share a message with you all." There was a gasp from the crowd and the jackrabbit held up his paws again and waited for them to settle back down.

"The raven wants us to know that he was sent by the Great Raven Spirit to help us through these troubling times; and that he will be at the rock by the trail to the waterhole tomorrow and every second morning at sunrise to share the Great Raven's message. We are all welcome to come and hear his message of hope and comfort."

For a moment the assembled creatures stared at the Elder in stunned silence, then the brush was filled with the buzz of excited conversations in every accent and tone common to the scrubland's communities.

The jackrabbit elder's announcement did not surprise Rabbit, but it did trouble her. It was particularly troubling in light of Tortoise's concerns. So, while the other creatures were excitedly discussing the raven's message, especially the part about "these troubling times", Rabbit was trying to decide what she should do next.

13

Coyote was lying in the shade by the pool in the juniper grove, unaware of the commotion caused by the news of the raven's visit. He had planned to go back to his den and nap for a while; but he changed his mind after meeting the raven and hearing his instructions. Instead, he was thinking hard about what he had just heard and what it meant for him.

Something about the raven's instructions made him uneasy. It wasn't that the raven had given him a task. In all the stories he had heard about ravens they assigned challenging tasks to the creatures they helped. It was the nature of his particular task that felt strange.

The stories told how ravens tested creatures by having them perform good deeds, like rescuing pups, or caring for ailing widows. Sometimes they sent the creatures off to live in isolation until they had a vision that could guide their choices. When the raven had spoken to him of what he must do to earn back his youth, those were the kinds of things he expected to hear. Instead, the raven had surprised him by assigning him to bring half of all his kills to a spot on the mesa every day at sundown and leave them there; then go directly back to his den and meditate on his youth until sunrise.

The raven explained that Coyote was to do this as a kind of personal offering, a sign of his faith, and a way of humbling himself before the spirits. He said that Coyote must continue this sacrifice until the next new moon; and he assured him that, if he was faithful, and pure of heart, the spirits would be pleased; they would accept his sacrifices; and they would return his youth to him.

When Coyote had asked the raven how he would know if the spirits were accepting his sacrifice as genuine, the raven told him that, if the sacrifices were gone when he brought fresh ones, then he would know that the spirits were looking favorably on them and on his efforts.

As Coyote turned to go, the Raven had warned him that the spirits would know if he was truly leaving their full offering. If they found that Coyote was not acting in good faith, they would withdraw their help and never offer it again; he would be doomed to remain old.

Coyote spent the rest of the morning lying motionless by the pool, his muzzle on his paws, thinking hard about what the raven had told him. It all seemed so strange, but the prospect of regaining his youth was too powerful to ignore. Finally, he swallowed his uneasiness and determined to follow the raven's instructions exactly.

The task would be challenging. Lately he had a difficult time making enough kills to keep himself fed; he could not afford to cut down his own meals by half; and that meant he would have to nearly double the kills he made each day. The prospect frightened him. What if he failed?

Clearly, that was the offering the raven had spoken about. His hard work and possible hunger would be the proof of his sincerity. The spirits would be pleased and they would grant his wish.

His mind was made up! He would not go back to his den and rest, even though he was very tired. Instead he would begin hunting and gather his first sacrifice before sundown today. He pulled his tired body up and headed back to his hunting trails.

A few hours later, just before sundown, a very tired Coyote walked slowly into a small clearing on the top of the mesa. He looked around warily and then carefully set two limp bodies on a flat slab of rock. He looked around once more, sighed and slowly walked back into the brush and, as the sun set, he headed down the slope toward his den.

If he had stayed behind to watch he would have seen a shadowy presence on four legs slip out of the deepening darkness, step up to the rock, scoop Coyote's offering up in white jaws and fade, quietly, back into the brush.

—

Rabbit had no idea what Coyote was up to; no hint of his connection to the raven's presence in the scrublands. Instead of keeping an eye on that "Silly Old Dog" she was methodically lingering on the edges of groups of creatures as they talked about the raven and the message it had sent. After a while she determined that, although many of the creatures were unsure of the meaning of the raven's words, all of them were excited at the prospect of hearing the raven speak and most of them were likely to turn up at the big rock tomorrow at dawn. She decided that she should be there to hear the raven's message first hand and to monitor the reaction of the crowd.

The next morning, Rabbit arrived at the big rock just before sunrise. At first she thought that she would be the only one there, but she was wrong. In a few minutes, creatures began arriving from every direction. By the time the first glimmer of light began to fill the eastern sky there were small creatures of every sort arrayed around the edges of the clearing; lizards, and tortoises, armadillos and mice, even a family of horned toads was there peering at the rock in anticipation from under the brush. A self-important old jackrabbit was hopping back in forth in front of the crowd telling them to be quiet and generally acting as though the raven's presence was personally arranged by his clan.

Just as the sun started to peak over the rim of the big rock and dazzle everyone's eyes, a large black figure appeared at the top and spread its wings. That great black shape was an impressive sight, looming above them, outlined in the blazing rays of the rising sun. The raven had arrived.

The crowd instantly became quiet. Even the bossy jackrabbit was stunned to silence. He crouched low, as though he were blocking the view and slipped into the bushes to stand with all the other creatures waiting to hear the raven speak.

The raven spent a few seconds looking at the crowd; then he began to speak in a harsh croaking voice.

"Thank you all for coming this morning. I am pleased to see so many of you here. I want to start by sending my condolences to the vole clan for their recent losses."

There was an audible gasp from the voles in the crowd. Just yesterday a group of them had been gathered discussing the raven's arrival when Coyote had charged out of the brush into the middle of them with a wild look in his eye, snapping and pouncing seemingly in all directions at once. By the time they had gotten over their initial shock and bolted for cover, four of them lay dead. As the rest watched in horrified silence, Coyote devoured two of them on the spot then picked up the other two and trotted away. How could the raven know about this?

Throughout the crowd, wherever they were standing, voles took a few steps forward into the open; drawn to be closer to the wonderful raven.

The raven went on to explain that their familiar Coyote had suddenly become voracious and turned into a wanton killer. He warned them "sadly" that these depredations would only become worse as time went on. A worried murmur broke out among the assembled creatures.

The raven waited a few seconds for the full impact of his words to sink in; then he exhorted them to be calm. He promised that he would work to protect them; that they would always be safe in his presence, and that he would intervene with the spirits on their behalf.

He finished by inviting them back to talk with him in two days. Then he asked them all to close their eyes as he croaked out an old, familiar blessing. When they opened them, the raven was gone.

Rabbit sat in stunned silence as all around her the creatures were chattering about the marvelous raven and the scourge of the mad Coyote.

Once Rabbit got over her surprise, she headed straight for Tortoise to share what she had learned and to get his counsel. He listened in grave silence has she told him about what the raven had said and of the impact it had on the assembled creatures, particularly on the voles.

Finally, when she had told him everything she knew, he shook his head and said "I have an idea what is going on but I am not certain. I have been hearing rumors of similar things happening in distant parts of the scrublands, particular up near the mountains."

"One thing is certain. You must keep a close watch on Coyote. My intuition tells me that he is the key to this puzzle. Watch him and see what he does. But be very careful. He is always dangerous, that is his nature;

but, something has happened, something connected to the raven. And, whatever it is has turned him into a ferocious killer. So, keep yourself safe at all costs."

Sigman Shapiro

14

Coyote knew nothing about the gathering at the rock. He had slept past midday, exhausted by the events of the preceding two days. Now he was standing just outside his den in the hot sun stretching and yawning, preparing for another grueling round of hunting for two.

At the same time, Rabbit was well hidden downwind in the bushes watching him. As he moved off into the brush to begin his hunt she followed him from a safe distance, being careful to move quietly and stay downwind.

This was the part of shadowing him that she hated. She knew he was going out to kill his dinner. She understood that coyotes were hunters and that killing was their role; their lot in life; she just hated having to watch it happen over and over again. No matter how many times she witnessed the moment of the kill, she couldn't stop her heart from racing in fear and could barely suppress her urge to shout a warning as he crept up on some small creature.

So far she had been lucky; for whatever reason, he had not chosen to hunt any of her relatives while she watched him. But she knew that was only coincidence, it was only a matter of time before he came across the opportunity for a rabbit dinner. For now though, she put that thought out of her mind and concentrated on staying close enough to know what he was doing yet far enough not to become a meal herself.

Coyote normally took his time hunting. He had his favorite spots, ones where he had the most luck in the past, and he would check in on some of them each day, being careful not to let his movements become predictable. However, today was different. Today he was hunting for more than a day's meal; he was hunting for his future.

Instead of his usual stealthy stroll, he trotted from place to place. He only gave a quick look at his usual spots then moved on to the next one. He took paths that he rarely traveled and poked his muzzle into burrows and bushes that, on other days, he would not have bothered checking.

Twice he came on groups of small creatures chattering and feeding in the brush. Both times he was just a split second too slow. As he pounced into their midst one of them would sound the alarm and they would all scatter in different directions, leaving him standing, alone in an empty clearing.

As the afternoon drew to a close he was starting to feel desperate. He was trotting down a narrow trail in thick scrub, it was one he seldom used. As he rounded a bend in the trail, he found a very large bull snake in the middle of the trail warming its body for the night's hunting. It was nearly as long as Coyote.

Shadow Season

THE SACRIFICE

The snake hadn't detected him yet, so Coyote paused for a second to think about what he should do. Even though they were competitors for the same prey, he usually wouldn't confront a creature like this; especially not one this size. His normal reaction would be to turn aside and circle around the snake without disturbing it.

Bull snakes are not poisonous, but it would be a ferociously powerful adversary. Even if he could subdue it, it might injure him bad enough that he couldn't hunt for a few days and that would ruin his chance to earn back his youth as the raven had promised.

However, if he could kill it, he could eat his fill and have more than half the carcass to bring as an offering to the spirits. The idea was very tempting. He decided it was too tempting to ignore; that he would risk it.

Coyote crouched down and crept toward the dozing snake. When he got within range he tensed his muscles and leapt toward the snake's head; but, once again, his reaction time was half a beat too slow. As he sprang toward his prey, the snake sensed him and, whipping itself into a coil, it turned with opened, hissing jaws to defy its attacker.

—
—

Rabbit was shocked and frightened when she saw Coyote attack the snake. After Coyote's initial lunge the two seemed almost frozen. Neither of them moved. The snake remained coiled and defiant. Coyote stood stiff-legged a few feet in front of it. Then, suddenly, Coyote lunged forward again and they were locked in a terrible struggle. The Snake had closed its jaws on the flesh under Coyote's neck and was wrapping itself around Coyote's ribs. Coyote had his teeth set into the middle of the snake's thick body and was shaking it violently from side to side.

At one point the snake managed to knock Coyote's legs from under him; then they were rolling back and forth in the dirt. Coyote was growling fiercely. He seemed half mad. The snake was silent but never stopped thrashing and delivering terrible blows to Coyote's body. Finally Coyote was able to shake the snake's jaws loose from his throat and quickly grab it just behind its head.

He began shaking the snake's head violently and pounding it on the ground. After a few minutes the snake went limp and its coils fell away from Coyote's body.

Rabbit could hear her heart pounding in her ears. She realized she had been holding her breath and she felt more than a little sick. She took deep breaths and tried to calm herself as she watched him stand there in the trail with the snake still in his jaws. His head was hanging down, he was panting and his legs were trembling so hard it looked unlikely he could stay on his feet.

Finally he seemed to pull himself together and he let the snake drop. It fell with a dull thud and did not move. It was clearly dead.

Coyote stared at it for a second; then he crouched down slowly, as if he was in pain, and started to devour his prey. He began at the tail and chewed and gnawed the flesh from the body, tearing off large chunks and swallowing them in gulps. When he had eaten almost half the snake, he stood up stiffly and took the remaining portion in his bloody jaws. He lifted his muzzle high and began to drag it down the trail with the head hanging down in the dirt.

Rabbit shook her head in wonder. This was clearly not the same Coyote she had been watching all these weeks. He was harder, fiercer, and much more dangerous than before. She had to find out what was behind this change and what part the raven had in it. As he disappeared around the bend in the trail, she fought down her nausea and waited until there was a safe distance between them; then she followed him to see what he would do next.

15

The fight with the snake had left Coyote exhausted. It had taken every ounce of strength in his old body. He was proud that he had succeeded; that he still had that much ferocity to call on if he needed it. He was also hurting.

Once the adrenalin wore off he began to feel just how badly he had been injured. His throat was torn where the snake had grabbed him, his ribs ached horribly with every breath, and his left hip seemed to be twisted so that he was limping on his left hind leg. He may have won the fight, but it had left him with a body full of pain.

He could see that the light was fading and knew that he would have to hurry if he was going to deliver his offering to the spirits before dark. So, he pushed his pain aside and began the trek up the backside of the mesa.

Rabbit followed a short way behind him as he limped down the trail dragging the snake. She couldn't figure out where he was going. This was not the way to his den. In fact, it was the opposite direction. She could tell he was hurting by the way he limped, but he never stopped, never slowed down. After a while she realized he was heading up onto the mesa. What could he possibly want up there? What was so important?

She followed him to the top of the mesa in the fading light. When he came to a small clearing she watched as he walked slowly into the center and dropped the carcass of the snake on a rock in the middle; then, as the last rays of the sun faded from the sky, he turned and walked away without looking back.

She sat there in the dark waiting for him to get far enough ahead so she could follow safely. She was trying to make sense of what she had seen; all that had happened. She watched him limp out of sight and was turning to follow when a movement in the clearing caught her eye. She stared into the gloom and what she saw almost made her forget her safety and gasp.

There was a creature creeping into the clearing. It came out of the brush quietly and picked up the body of the snake then slipped back into the brush in the opposite direction of Coyote's exit. She realized this was the key to the whole mystery; so, instead of following Coyote back to his den, she followed this new creature to see where it was going and what it would do.

—
—

Coyote had spent a miserable night. As soon as he limped into his den he collapsed and fell into a deep sleep driven by physical exhaustion; then, after an hour or two his aches and pains began to weigh more on him than his need for sleep and he tossed and turned trying to find any position that would ease his discomfort.

A few hours before dawn his exhaustion won and he finally fell back into a kind of half sleep. He was settling deeper into welcome rest when he heard a small voice calling his name. "Wake up Coyote! Wake Up!" it said. He fought to stay asleep, but the voice insisted. He knew if he wanted to be left alone, he was going to have to answer it. He lifted his aching head from his paws and said, "What do you want?" in a grumpy voice heavy with sleep.

"The raven sent me." was the answer.

At the mention of the raven Coyote was instantly awake. As he struggled to get to his feet he said "What does he want?"

The voice said "He wants you to come to the rock a little before sunrise. Stay out of sight and pay attention. He wants you to see what happens. Do you understand? Will you be there?"

"Yes. I understand. I will be there." he replied.

He started toward the entrance to his den to get a look at this messenger but his wounded old body moved too slowly. When he poked his nose out the entrance, the creature was gone. So, he staggered back to his bed and plopped down with a groan. He didn't dare go back to sleep now or he'd sleep through the appointment. Instead, he laid still and tried to rest.

Rabbit left Coyote's den as soon as she was sure he understood her message. She had a long way to go and would have to hurry if she was going to get there in time.

She ran down the dark trail as fast as she could. The moonless sky meant the stars were gleaming brightly overhead. Her eyes were adapted to see in the dark, still, she was glad for the extra light. She finally reached her destination about an hour before sunrise. She hid in the bushes outside an abandoned badger den and waited.

After a while she saw a white muzzle poke out of the old den and sniff the air cautiously. It was followed by the oldest dog she had ever seen. His face was entirely white and the fur on his body was mostly gray. His legs were spindly and looked far too thin to support his round belly. "He may be old, but he is certainly well fed!" she thought.

The dog yawned and did some quick stretches, then he stuck his nose back into the badger den and dragged out what looked like a pile of dusty, old, black feathers. As she watched, he proceeded to wriggle under the pile until he had draped himself in the feathers; they covered his back and there were even ragged sleeves that covered his front legs and looked like wings.

Finally, he stuck his nose behind some bushes and pulled out a crude headdress made of feathers and old animal bones. The only part uncovered was his long, gray tail; it stuck out behind him like a flag.

When his preparations were complete he rose up on his hind legs, and hopped in a clumsy fashion to a small puddle nearby to check his reflection. He made a few small adjustments to his strange costume until he seemed satisfied. "Perfect" she heard him say in a croaky kind of voice; then he turned and began to hop again.

Rabbit had expected she would see something like this; still the transformation stunned her. He didn't really look like a raven; but he didn't look like a dog either.
She realized he was counting on the fact that ravens were incredibly rare here to help him fool all the scrubland creatures.

In fact, only two creatures in the area actually had ever seen a raven. One was Tortoise. He had seen a raven and heard it speak many years ago when he was young. He had told the story countless times in the years since and it always wowed the youngsters and quite a few of their parents too.

The other creature who had seen a real raven and heard it speak was Rabbit; but she never mentioned it to anyone. It was part of her vision quest and, therefore, not something to be chattered about.

The "raven" hopped out of the grove and through the brush with rabbit trailing behind. He hopped and hopped until he came to the back side of the big rock by the clearing. He waited there until the sun just began to peek over the horizon; then he hopped up onto the rock; squatted back to hide his tail behind him, spread his "wings" wide, and began to make croaking sounds. Rabbit lingered out of sight nearby waiting for the right moment to act.

—

From where she was hidden Rabbi could see dozens and dozens of animals gathered on the edge of the clearing. They were standing in awed silence; as if in the presence of some great creature; and they had even brought their young ones.

The dog waited for a second, surveying the crowd through the slits in his headdress, then he began to talk to them in his croaky "raven" voice. After a while, when he had his audience enthralled, he began to drop his voice a bit. It was subtle at first, but gradually the creatures surrounding him were edging a little closer in order to hear. Every few seconds he spoke a bit softer, and every few seconds the rats, and voles, the mice and prairie dogs, and all the other creatures took a few wide-eyed steps closer to what they thought was a raven on the rock.

Rabbit watched this performance in wonder. The dog would croak softly and the creatures would move forward; then he would speak lower and they would move even closer. "Well", Rabbit thought, "if he keeps this up they'll be practically standing on his toes in no time". In that instant a vision flashed through Rabbit's mind. She saw dozens of trusting prey standing quietly, in awe at the "raven's" feet, hypnotized by his voice.

She had planned to expose him for what he was, but this was the part of her plan that she hadn't quite worked out yet. What could she do? Her voice was too quiet to be effective at spreading an alarm; and she wasn't sure they'd believe her anyway. They were far too enthralled by the "raven" to listen to her.

Then she had an idea. It was a desperate plan, but she knew it was the only way.

She raced around behind the rock in a wide circle, keeping out of sight. The dog and his avid listeners were too caught up in their deadly game to notice her anyway. When she got directly behind him she dashed up and grabbed his bushy gray tail in her teeth and gave it a powerful tug; then she raced off shouting "Hey old dog! Who do you think you are fooling?"

The effect was immediate. The dog whirled around in anger; ready to pounce on the creature who dared to touch his tail and to insult him in such a coarse way! As he spun around his bushy tail was in full view of all the creatures gathered at the foot of the rock. For an instant they were stunned and confused. Then a young ground squirrel said what they all were thinking, "Why does the raven have a dog's tail?" In an instant they all knew they had been tricked!

With a squeal, almost as one creature, everyone turned and scattered as fast as they could for cover. By the time the dog realized his mistake and turned back around, no one was there but Coyote.

Coyote was standing, trembling in the clearing looking up at the rock in confusion. He had expected to see a sacred raven, a messenger of the spirits. Instead, what he saw was an old, gray dog standing there under a pile of dusty bird feathers glaring at him. Then, without warning, Coyote leaped for the top of the rock!

Rabbit raced away from the old impostor as fast as she could. When she reached the cover of the brush she turned to check on her pursuer. She was surprised to find that he was not chasing her at all; instead, he was standing on the rock confronting a very fierce, angry Coyote.

Rabbit had never seen Coyote like this; he was standing tall and stiff-legged; his fur was all on end. Rabbit could hear his low, menacing growl and he was baring his long fangs.

In spite Coyote's threats, the dog was not backing down. His vision was limited by his mask and his movements were impaired by being wrapped in his long feathery cape; but he still met Coyote's growls with snarls of defiance.

They stood there for what seemed like minutes. It was as if they were frozen. Then the dog began inching slowly to the left to get a more favorable line of attack.

His eyes were locked with Coyote's; watching for the slightest flicker of warning that he would spring.

Rabbit watched horrified as the two fierce predators circled slowly on the rock. Then the dog's foot became tangled in his feather cape. His concentration was broken for a second and he faltered. As he tried to regain his balance, his hind leg stepped off the edge of the rock.

Coyote saw the expression in the dog's eyes change from defiance to surprise. That was the opening he was waiting for. He leaped toward him and sank his teeth into his adversary's throat. The blow knocked the dog backward and the two of them tumbled off the rock and landed hard in a cloud of dust on the ground below.

Coyote was stunned by the fall and he momentarily loosened his grip on the dog's throat. The dog yelped and, fueled by terror, he used all his strength to shake Coyote loose from his torn and bleed neck; then he turned tail and ran as fast as he could off into the brush leaving a trail of feathers behind him as his cloak caught on the scrub and was pulled apart.

Coyote was embarrassed. He had been tricked by a dog! A dog! The shame was too much. He could not let the vile creature get away with it; not if he was ever going to hold up his head in the scrublands again. He took a deep breath and shook his head; then took off after him.

Sigman Shapiro

16

Coyote left his den in the pre-dawn, and headed out to hunt up some breakfast. He passed his usual hunting trails and trotted further out into the open scrubland. In about an hour he was scouting along the extreme eastern edge of his hunting grounds.

The scrubland was a hard place to survive. Prey was not abundant and he had always ranged over a wide territory to find enough to eat. He preferred to stay closer to home but, lately, he had not had much success on his usual routes; so there he was, tracing an old track through the brush, hoping to find an unwary rodent or a sleepy lizard.

By late morning he hadn't had any luck; in fact, he hadn't encountered any other creatures at all. That is, until he stepped into a small clearing and there, on the opposite edge, was another coyote.

The coyote was male. He looked ancient and seemed to be in a very poor state. His fur was all gray around his muzzle. His tail was ratty, as though most of the hair had fallen out. His head drooped; and he was mumbling to himself. He didn't seem to notice Coyote at first.

Coyote was about to withdraw quietly and leave him undisturbed, then the old fellow looked up and realized that he had company. He bowed to Coyote in the traditional greeting of their kind. Coyote bowed back politely and they approached each other. There followed the usual canine sniffing and posturing as they established their identities and verified that neither of them was going to threaten the other.

When the greeting ritual was over, Coyote realized with a start that he knew this old fellow. It was his brother! They were litter mates! He may look old and on his last legs, but he was not one day older than Coyote himself! How could his brother have aged so much when he, Coyote, was still so young?

He put these thoughts aside and called him by name. His brother looked at him for a second and then yelped with joy. At his insistence, they trotted over to a shady spot to settle down and do some catching up.

At first their conversation was the usual sort in these situations. They reminisced about the good times in their childhood den. They spoke of parents and siblings, of past mates and the litters they had helped to raise. Through it all, Coyote couldn't stop wondering why his brother had aged so quickly. He wanted to ask him about it, but wasn't sure how to bring it up without offending him. Finally, he just blurted it out. "You don't look well. You've aged so fast. What happened to you?"

His brother looked at him for a second, and then he chuckled and shook his head. "I was thinking the same thing about you. Neither of us is young any more. Time seems to be catching up with us"; then he became very quiet, very pensive. Coyote asked him what was troubling him. His brother stared at the ground, as though he was trying to decide whether to share a secret; then he began to speak.

"I have been having a very unsettling experience lately. I keep seeing a shadow wherever I go. It is always lurking in the corner of my left eye. But, when I turn to look at it directly, it is gone.

It started a few months ago. At first I only saw it now and then. I thought maybe I was tired; I do feel tired a lot lately. I thought it would go away if I rested more. But, instead; it has become more and more frequent until, now, it is there almost all the time.

I think something is following me; but I don't know why. I have tried hiding and waiting to see if I can catch it; but that never works. I have tried turning suddenly and shouting at it; challenging it to show itself. So far, I have had no luck.

I have a hard time sleeping now, because I don't know what it wants. I am afraid it will come after me when I am asleep. I can't concentrate because I am exhausted and beside myself with worry; and I can't hunt because I can't concentrate."

Coyote Looked at him and asked "Can I help in some way?" His brother's eyes lit up at the offer and he said "Yes, I think you can!" and he went on to explain his plan.

They would meet again tomorrow early in the day and spend the day hunting together. It would be like old times except for one thing, the real reason for the "hunt" would be to capture the "Shadow Creature".

His brother would go off on his usual hunting rounds as though nothing were happening. Coyote would follow after a while and trail him at a safe distance, out of sight. If they worked it right, Coyote should be able to creep up behind the creature and pounce on it before it realized he was there.

It seemed like a good plan to Coyote. He agreed that he would meet his brother under some pinion trees near the dry arroyo an hour or so after sunrise; then they parted and headed back to their hunting.

—

Rabbit had checked in on Coyote that morning; it was something she had begun to do a while ago, checking in to see what he was up to.

Today, as usual, she followed him as he began his rounds, but he didn't take any of his regular routes; instead, he headed out east toward the far edges of his territory.

After half an hour of this she stopped and thought "What is that Silly Old Dog up to now? There is no way I am going to spend my day trudging out to the end of nowhere."

After thinking it over, she decided he would be fine on his own. She made a mental note to check on him again late in the day and turned back to spend some time doing rabbit sorts of things.

—
—

Coyote tried to go back to his hunting after he left his brother but had no luck. He found he couldn't concentrate. He couldn't stop thinking about his brother's words "Neither of us is young any more. Time seems to be catching up with us". That thought made him very uncomfortable; so uncomfortable that he lost his appetite. Finally, in the late afternoon, he gave up in frustration and headed back toward home.

On the way to his den he came to the trail to the juniper grove and the small pool that he loved. He decided to turn that way and spend some time resting and thinking in the shade.

When he got to the pool he looked around. "Good", he thought, "There's no one here. I can be alone." He walked to the edge of the pool, took a drink, then flopped down in a shady spot to ponder the day's events.

It had been very unsettling to see his brother, who was once so fierce and fearless, so frightened of a shadow.

Even more unsettling was his brother's remark about aging. He had thought hard about it and, though they were actually the same age, he was sure that he did not look as old as his brother. Just to be sure, he got up and leaned out over the pond, tilting his head from side to side as he examined his reflection in its still water.

"No," he muttered, "I don't see it."

$$-$$

Rabbit had spent her day cleaning out her burrow, catching up with her rabbit friends, and giving her ears a good grooming. All in all it had been a very satisfying day and a well-needed break.

As sunset approached she hopped over toward Coyote's den to check in on him. When she got there she listened, sniffed and watched from her usual spots and realized he was not home. So, she headed for the juniper pond, since it was the next most likely place to find him.

She was careful to approach the pond from down wind and to stay concealed – even old coyotes were, after all, dangerous for rabbits.

Sure enough, as she peeked out from behind a large clump of bunchgrass, she saw him by the water. He was lying on his belly with his head resting on his front paws and he had a far away look in his eyes – as though he was lost in thought, trying to figure something out.

She nodded to herself and was pleased to see she had guessed right. Clearly nothing had happened today that she needed to be aware of. She gave a last glance in his direction then headed back to her burrow for a bit of dinner. She was looking forward to a night of rabbit socializing. She had been so busy and tired, it would be the first she had had since she took responsibility for the Old Dog.

—
—

Coyote laid by the pond thinking and fretting until the stars came out and the night turned cold; then he got up and trotted back to his den still mulling the day over in his mind.

The next morning, after a restless night, he woke before dawn and, remembering his commitment to his brother, he trotted off to the pinion grove to meet him and begin their hunt for the mysterious Shadow Creature. He didn't rush. He was sure he'd have to wait for a while when he got there. When they were young his brother was known for never being on time. Coyote figured he could use the extra time to try and scrounge up a bite in the nearby arroyo.

Coyote was surprised to find his brother there waiting when he trotted up. He was even more surprised to find his brother had captured a bit of breakfast and was waiting to share it with him.

While they ate their snack, his brother went over the plan again. He would head out first. They would hunt for food (of course) but they would really be hunting for the mysterious Shadow Creature.

When he saw that the creature was following him, he would turn and shout at it and Coyote, who would be trailing him by a few minutes, would know to rush up and nab his stalker.

All the time they were eating and talking Coyote noticed that his brother kept glancing nervously over his shoulder, as though he was being watched.

Rabbit woke that morning feeling very rested. She yawned and stretched and then had a bite to eat. When she looked at the stars she could tell that sunrise was not far off; so she quickly tidied up her fur and washed her ears, then she hurried over to Coyote's den. She barely arrived in time to see him disappear down the trail headed east.

She thought it was odd that he would go back toward where he had been yesterday, but she had no time to ponder the meaning of it all; she had to hurry if she was going to keep up with his long legs.

She followed him for an hour at a safe distance. By the way he traveled she could tell he was not hunting. He was clearly headed for a destination, but what could he possibly want out here? Then she saw him enter the pinion grove and meet up with another coyote who was every bit as old as him.

She could see them talking and eating but could not quite catch what they were saying. She could hear more if she got closer, but it was one thing to be close to one coyote; it was another to be close to two of them! So she stayed where she was and tried to interpret their actions.

—
—

Once they had finished their snack, Coyote's brother moved to leave. As he reached the edge of the clearing he looked over his shoulder as if he was ensuring that Coyote really would be there for him. He nodded and then adopted a nose to ground hunting posture as he slipped off into the brush.

Coyote waited for a while, then, when he thought his brother was far enough ahead, he set off after him. As they had agreed, his brother left a clear trail so he had no problem slipping along in his track; being careful to move quietly and conceal his presence.

As he trotted along Coyote kept thinking about his brother; what he was doing, how strange he was acting. Something about the whole situation made him very uncomfortable, he was beginning to think his brother had stayed out in the sun too long, or maybe he had eaten something that affected his brain.

His musings were interrupted when he heard his brother yip then growl fiercely just ahead. That was the signal! He had seen the creature!

Coyote moved swiftly toward the sounds. When he was close he could see his brother standing stiff-legged in a small clearing. His fur was all bristled and he was staring off slightly to the left as though confronting a threat. Coyote was too experienced to barge into the clearing head on; instead, he circled around toward the left to surprise his prey from an unexpected angle.

When he reached a large boulder roughly in line with his brother's snarling stare he crept up the back side and, just before he reached the top, he leaped down onto the ground where his brother's eyes were focused.

He hit the ground a bit harder than he expected and his old legs failed him. He tumbled and rolled, then quickly scrambled to his feet. He looked around from side to side, but there was nothing there; no Shadow Creature; not even any tracks in the soft, sandy dirt except his own.

He had missed! The creature had escaped.

Rabbit watched the two coyotes separate and move off into the brush a few minutes apart. It was clear they were on the hunt for something. She realized they must be related. Everyone knew that coyotes do not hunt together unless they are family. She had no idea Coyote had family nearby. She was curious to see what they were up to. So she waited for them to get a safe distance ahead, then she followed them into the brush.

Shadow Season

THE BROTHERS

She hadn't been following them for more than a few minutes when she heard a raucous snarling and growling. Her natural instincts told her to turn tail now and run as fast as she could to some place safe. It's what any normal, intelligent rabbit would do. But she was no normal rabbit. She was responsible for Coyote, and that meant she had to know what was gong on.

So, even though her heart was pounding and her legs were trembling, she hopped quietly on toward the sounds. She arrived just in time to see Coyote pick himself up off the ground, shake his head and stare all around as though he were dazed, then he trotted out into the clearing where the other coyote was standing, looking wildly about and trembling.

Coyote stood for a second staring at the ground all around him; then he looked back into the clearing. He saw his brother looking frightened and bewildered, as though he had lost something. Coyote sighed then walked slowly into the clearing and up to him. He could see that his brother was completely terrified. He nuzzled him and spoke softly to him in a calm and reassuring voice. Gradually, he talked him down until he was able to make eye contact and recognize that Coyote was with him.

They moved to a small patch of shade, sat, and talked about what had just happened and what was the best way to proceed. Coyote asked his brother if he had even been close to pouncing on their prey. His brother admitted that he hadn't seen anything once he turned to confront the creature. It was always like this. He would turn and threaten, only to find that the creature had slipped away before he could get a good look at it.

Coyote reassured him that the creature's days were numbered. With two seasoned hunters like them on its trail, it was only a matter of time before it would be caught and eliminated. He reminded his brother of their exploits as youngsters; how they had been widely feared and respected for their ability to hunt as a team. His brother smiled and thanked him for being there. They agreed to meet and try again the next day; then they parted, each heading back to his own den.

As he trotted home, Coyote thought over the events of the morning. He was perplexed. He couldn't believe he had missed the creature so completely. He had had a lot of trouble with his eyes lately and had missed more than one meal because of it, but this was different. This was not a skittery lizard or jumpy kangaroo rat. His brother had assured him this was a large and threatening creature. There was no way he should have missed it.

He stopped for a second and looked back over his shoulder. "I should have checked the area more carefully for tracks" he thought, "I could at least have figured out what sort of creature we are dealing with." For a moment he thought about turning back to investigate; then something told him it would be a waste of time; besides, he was suddenly very tired and his stomach was complaining. He hadn't eaten more than a snack all day. So, he pointed his nose toward home and headed back to rest up for tomorrow's hunt.

Rabbit watched the two coyotes meet in the clearing and talk, then separate. This did not seem like a usual hunt. It seemed very strange to her that they would stop so abruptly after such a short time. And, what were they hunting after all? There was no sign of any other creature, in spite of the dramatic posturing she had witnessed. All she could see were two very old coyotes behaving like two "Silly Old Dogs".

As Coyote turned toward home, she headed out in a wide circle that would keep her a safe distance from him yet allow her to intersect him about midway on the trail back to their part of the scrubland.

When she got near the trail, she waited in the brush and watched as he passed. He was mumbling to himself and seemed to be quite agitated. She fell in behind him and tried to get close enough to hear his words while keeping a safe distance. After a while he stopped in his tracks and glanced back in her direction. She froze and her heart pounded. Had he seen her?

No, apparently not. He shook his head as if changing his mind, then turned back toward home and continued down the trail.

Something unusual was going on, she wasn't sure what it was, but she knew she needed to find out. When they approached his den she made a note to be back there bright and early tomorrow to keep an eye on him. She watched as he crawled inside his den; then headed for her own snug burrow.

The next three days were almost exact copies of the first hunt. Coyote got up early and went to the pinion grove where his brother was waiting. They talked a bit and then headed out to hunt for the Shadow Creature. At some point Coyote's brother would raise the alarm and Coyote would rush in to pounce on their prey; only to find no sign of the creature. No matter how Coyote varied his approach, he could never catch the beast that was causing his brother so much distress.

At first he blamed himself for their failure. He knew he had been having trouble hunting for a while. His eyesight was not as good as it once was; and his speed and agility were not up to snuff lately. Clearly the creature was outwitting and out maneuvering him.

By the third day, however, he began to have doubts that they would ever catch their elusive prey. What kind of creature could hunt his brother but leave no trace; not a track, not even a scent? Was the Shadow Creature really there, or was there something wrong with his brother?

He began to observe his brother closely, not with loving eyes, but objectively, and what he saw worried him a lot. Every time they missed their prey his brother seemed to sink deeper into despair. He was not eating or sleeping well. His body was getting thinner; almost skin and bones. He was not grooming himself; his fur became more and more ragged and dirty each day. When they talked he seemed less and less present; his ramblings were becoming harder to follow, less coherent.

Coyote had promised his brother he would help him, but what they were doing was not helping; instead it seemed his brother was being rapidly destroyed by the whole process. He needed to find some other way to keep his promise. He needed to find some other kind of help.

Each night as he lay in his den he thought about the day's events and tried to think of a way to help. On the fourth night he remembered when he was still a pup; their mother had told him about Tortoise. "Tortoise is the oldest and wisest creature on the Scrubland" she said, "If you are ever in trouble; ever need advice; go to him. He will know what to do."

When Coyote woke on the fifth morning, he knew what he had to do. He would confront his brother and, somehow, convince him to go talk to Tortoise about this shadow he kept seeing. If anyone could help his brother find his way back to reality it would be Tortoise.

Now that he had a plan, he felt much better, more hopeful. He set off toward the pinion grove with a lighter heart and a quicker step. He was anxious to talk sense to his brother and get him on the path to recovery.

Rabbit had been trailing along behind the two coyotes for the past four days watching them as they went through the routine of their "hunt". By creeping close and listening intently, she had managed to pick up some idea of what they were doing.

Just as she had guessed, they were related, the other "Silly Old Dog" was Coyote's brother. Apparently there was some sort of creature that was stalking him and Coyote was trying to help him catch it; but they were not having any luck. In fact, the only one who ever saw the creature was Coyote's brother.

By the third time they acted out their silly charade, Rabbit had figured out that there was no creature to catch. It appeared to her that Coyote's brother was not well; not physically, and certainly not mentally. She wondered if Coyote knew what was going on and, if not, how long it would take him to figure it out.

Now, on the fifth morning, he was heading out to the "hunt" one more time. As soon as he turned down the trail to the pinion grove, she knew where he was going. She circled around him and hopped quickly toward the grove so she could be there when he arrived.

What she saw when she got there caused her to stop and stare; almost forgetting to hide for safety.

Sigman Shapiro

As Coyote trotted toward the meeting with his brother, he rehearsed his arguments in his head. One by one he imagined his brother's objections and, one by one, he crafted his responses till he was certain his plan could not fail.

When he arrived at the edge of the clearing he instinctively stopped and looked around. There was his brother waiting across the small open space waiting in the shade as usual. There he was, but something wasn't right.

Coyote stood very still trying to understand what was wrong; then he knew. His brother was there resting peacefully under the tree, but he was not breathing.

He was dead.

Coyote felt a shiver run through him from the tip of his nose to the tip of his tail. He lowered his head and walked slowly over to his brother's body.

Rabbit saw Coyote step to the edge of the clearing; then stop and shiver. He whimpered softly, lowered his head, walked sadly to his brother's body, and sat beside him; then he raised his muzzle into the sky, and let out with the longest, saddest howl she had ever heard.

17

Coyote groaned and opened his eyes. He looked around his den and sighed wearily. The last few days had been hard. Whether he was awake or asleep he could not stop thinking about, dreaming about, his brother; their times together as young pups; their last days together spent hunting the Shadow Creature. He could not shake his deep sadness and guilt, not just for the loss of his brother, but for his own inability to save him. Beneath his sadness was something else, something even more unsettling than his guilt. Beneath his sadness was a tiny seed of fear.

All the emotional turmoil had left him strangely weak; unable to find the will to move. He had even lost his appetite; something that had never happened before. He lay in his den day after day and, in between bouts of mourning, he wondered how he would ever find the strength to step out into the world; how he would ever hunt again; that is, until today.

Today his empty belly was louder than his roiling thoughts. He was hungry; too hungry to ignore. So, he pulled himself up onto his feet and, slowly stepping out into the open, he lifted his nose and sniffed the air for the first time in days.

Rabbit had been lingering outside Coyote's den for several days, ever since she had witnessed his shock at the death of his brother. She had seen him that day as he left his brother's body in the shade of the pinions; she had seen him stop at the edge of the clearing and look back; seen how he looked up at the slow gyre of vultures as they circled in the clear sky waiting for him to leave. She watched him shake his head in resignation, then turn and head back down the trail toward his den.

She had followed him home that day and she had been keeping watch outside his den ever since; only leaving to satisfy the demands of sleep and hunger. She stayed near him in the hope that she would find a way to help him ease his pain.

His sorrow had obviously been terrible. She had heard him as he whimpered and groaned hour after hour. She could hear his soft growls, his sharp cries, and the kicking of his legs as he fought the Shadow Creature in his dreams.

Each day she grew more worried. What if she failed him? What if he never came out of his den? What if he simply faded and died in this terrible sorrow? Finally, it had been too much for her and she had hopped off to see Tortoise; to ask for his help.

She found her old master in his usual spot, half buried in the loose dirt, dozing in the shade of the pinion.

She approached him and softly called his name. He opened his eyes and blinked then stretched his legs one by one. Finally, he looked at her and shook his head. "Something is troubling you Rabbit", he said. "What is wrong?"

Rabbit moved closer so he could hear her; he was a bit deaf in one ear. When she was close enough, she settled down in the shade near him and began to tell him about Coyote; how he and his brother went hunting for the Shadow Creature; how Coyote's brother had died; and about Coyote's terrible grief ever since.

Tortoise listened patiently, nodding his head from time to time. Finally, when she was silent, he looked at her and said, "Coyote must mourn his brother. It is a real loss, and he must mourn that loss in his own way. We can not interfere with that. It will be what it must be. You can watch and feel compassion, but you can not spend your energy there."

"Instead, you must prepare yourself; something is coming that will shake him deeper than even the loss of his brother. Soon he will need you more than ever. When it happens, you will know it. It is the reason the Great Mother called you to help him."

"When it happens, you must find a way to guide him to me. You are young; Coyote is old. Someday you will be old and you will know what Coyote is facing. Until then, he must hear the truth from one who is old and has seen what he will see."

"This does not mean there is any lack in you. It takes great wisdom to know when to call on others for help. I can lay the truth before him; but, in the end, it is you who have been chosen to guide his spirit to peace."

—

Coyote stood outside his den for a while letting his eyes adjust to the autumn light. He felt weak and disoriented. He hadn't realized until then how long it had been since he had eaten. His belly was complaining non-stop. He was going to have to find some food right away.

He sniffed the breeze, letting his nose do the hunting and, in a short time he had located something he could eat. No coyote would turn down a bit of carrion when they were truly hungry; and he was truly hungry. So, he slowly headed off toward some breakfast on wobbly legs.

Later, after a small snack, he headed to his favorite spot by the juniper pool to get some water and to let his food digest. He was feeling stronger now, but he was still not up to par.

—

Since her talk with Tortoise, Rabbit had been even more diligent in watching over Coyote. She barely ever left her post outside his den day or night. She had even set aside some of her natural caution and had begun to position herself dangerously close to his den.

She was becoming exhausted by her vigil and was almost nodding off when he decided to leave his den. The first warning she got was when she heard his breathing and saw the tip of his nose emerge from the entrance. Suddenly she was wide awake, her heart was racing with a realization of danger and, instinctively, she jumped and ran to cover. By the time he had stepped out into the open on his wobbly legs and sniffed the air, she was back down wind and watching from a safe spot, smiling to herself. She was glad to see the silly old dog had ended his isolation.

When he slowly headed off to get some food, she waited for a bit: then followed at a safe distance.

—
—

Coyote was on his way to the little juniper pool when something caught his attention. It was a hint of movement off to the left; barely visible in the corner of his eye. When he turned to see what it was, there was nothing there. He didn't think much of it. The sunlight frequently cast strange shadows out here in the scrublands. He quickly dismissed it and continued on his way.

Later, as he stopped at the end of the trail and checked things out before proceeding to the pond, he got the same sense that he had seen something moving at the far left edge of his field of vision; and again, when he looked directly where it had been, there was nothing there. Normally he would have been more curious; would have trusted his senses and investigated. But, right now, he was too tired and too preoccupied to spend the energy. Instead, he ambled over to the inviting coolness of the pool and settled down in his favorite spot to lap up some water, rest and think.

Think! It seemed like that was all he did these days. Here he was, stretched out in his favorite spot; he should be resting, soaking up peace and feeling content. Instead, he was thinking about his brother. There was something about that whole episode that left him feeling very uneasy; something he was supposed to remember, what was it?

Normally his thinking never strayed far from how to get his next meal; but, lately (since his brother died) he'd been thinking a lot about his own life; what he was doing, why he was doing it. It made him uncomfortable; all this thinking; and it scared him a little too. Then he saw it again; the movement in the far corner of his left eye.

He felt a rush of fear shake him. In an instant he was on his feet and staring toward where the shadow had been. Yes! It was a shadow! The Shadow Creature! Was this the elusive presence that his brother had sworn was hunting him in the days before he died?

Coyote had never actually seen the creature; though he had spent hours helping his brother hunt it. His brother had insisted that it was real in spite of their failure to see any solid evidence. Eventually, Coyote had come to believe that it was imaginary; a symptom of some kind of sickness his brother was battling. Now he was seeing it himself!

He stood and stared at the corner of the small clearing. His fur was standing on end and he was growling low and baring his teeth. He moved slowly on stiffened legs toward the spot where it had been. When he got there, there was no sign any creature had been there. Just like the days he and his brother hunted it together, the creature seemed able to move about without leaving any tracks, no scent, no sign at all!

Coyote was no coward, but now, he found himself unable to stop shaking. Raw fear was replacing his anger. He looked wildly about, trying to see where his enemy might lie in wait. No matter where he looked, there was no sign of the creature. Finally, his tail drooped between his legs and he let go a whimper; then he turned and raced wildly down the trail toward his den.

Rabbit had followed Coyote to his spot by the juniper pool and found a safe and comfortable vantage point. She was glad to see him returning to his old, favorite spots. It seemed things were taking a positive turn for him. Even so, she could not relax completely, could not forget Tortoise's words "...something is coming that will shake him deeper than even the loss of his brother".

Still, right now things seemed peaceful enough and she felt great relief after the days spent in anxious vigil outside his den. She even allowed herself the luxury of a yawn and stretch; certain that he could not see her.

She was thinking about grooming her ears when it happened. Coyote whipped his head to the left and in an instant he was on his feet growling and snarling at something across the pool from where she was hiding. She looked hard where he was staring, but could not see what had upset him.

When he moved toward an empty patch of grass bank, she realized she had seen this behavior before. It was the way Coyote's brother had acted when he thought he had seen the imaginary Shadow Creature! Surely the silly old dog was not going to succumb to that illusion!

When she saw him turn in an instant from a fierce predator to a quivering, whimpering beast, when she saw him tuck his tail between his legs and flee in terror from an imaginary threat, she knew her worst fear was true. Coyote had gone mad, just like his brother.

Coyote spent the next few days hiding in his den. He only came out at night to grab a quick bite and a bit of water. He had tried coming out in the daylight, but he always caught a glimpse of the Shadow Creature and ran back inside.

Unlike his brother, he had made no further attempts to confront his enemy. He knew from experience how futile that would be. Instead, he holed up and fretted over what to do, how to escape his brother's fate.

Day or night, his moans and whimpers could be heard for some distance outside his den.

Rabbit had returned to her post outside Coyote's den. The vigil was beginning to wear her out. She realized she was very worried about him, in spite of him being her natural enemy.

Hour after hour she sat and thought about what to do. Tortoise had said "When it happens, you must find a way to guide him to me" but how in the world was she going to do that?

He never came out in the day time and, even if he did, he was certainly not going to take advice from her. To him she was just lunch. The whole challenge weighed on her thoughts, and the more she thought about it, the more hopeless it seemed.

On the third day she was close to giving up. Just before sunset, sad and exhausted, she hopped home to her snug burrow and settled in for a fitful night's sleep.

While she slept she dreamed. At first her dreams were the usual dreams of a young rabbit, but then everything changed. She found herself walking through the scrub with Tortoise. He was showing her where to find a special plant. He called it the Dream Bush.

As they moved down the trail, Tortoise explained the steps she must take to help Coyote. He told her how she must use the plant to help her remain awake while she was dreaming. He also explained how she could visit Coyote and enter his dreams. He said, "If you appear to him in a familiar and trusted shape, he will listen to you and you can guide him." His words seemed strange, but she understood what he was telling her.

When they arrived at the Dream Bush he told her to study it carefully, but not to taste it. She sniffed it (it had a strong medicinal scent) and looked at the leaves closely. She realized she had seen this sort of shrub many times before. She also remembered that her mother had pointed it out when she was very young and had warned her that it would make her sick and she must never eat it.

Tortoise was watching her. When he was satisfied she could recognize it again he nodded and said, "You must remember what I have told you when you wake up. It is very important." She nodded to him and everything faded to black.

The next morning she woke slowly in her own bed. As she laid there, half way between sleep and waking, she recalled every detail of the strange dream as though it had actually happened; as though her mind had been walking through the scrublands with Tortoise while her body remained asleep here in her burrow.

She was fully awake in an instant. The memory of the dream excited her and she decided to go looking for the Dream Bush to see if it was really where she had dreamed it was.

She hopped out of her burrow without even grooming her ears and looked around. She realized she wasn't sure which way to go. For a second she was confused; then she quieted her mind and the answer came to her.

She hopped off through the brush until she came to the foot of a small shrub. Yes, it was the Dream Bush from her dream. She looked around on the ground to see if there was any sign that she and Tortoise had been there. The only tracks were the ones she had just made. She shook her head in wonder and then gathered a few of the fresh leaves as Tortoise had instructed, and hopped back to her burrow.

She spent another day watching outside Coyote's den and thinking over the instructions she had received from Tortoise in her dream. He had told her she would need something that had belonged to Coyote; something that would help her focus her mind on him to the exclusion of all other distractions.

At first she was unsure what that would be. Then she noticed a tuft of his fur hanging from the tip of a branch outside his den. "Of course!" she thought. "What could belong to Coyote more than his own fur?" She spent an hour moving along the trails near his den, collecting bits of his fur.

At the end of the day, she settled into her bed with the leaves from the Dream Bush and Coyote's fur within reach and cleared her mind of all thoughts just as Tortoise had taught her. When she felt ready, she began chewing the leaves from the Dream Bush as she focused all her thoughts on Coyote and held his fur to her nose and inhaled his scent as an aid to concentration.

After a short time the leaves took effect and she felt her body gradually drifting off into a deep sleep while her mind remained alert and active. She was ready to do what Tortoise had called Dream Walking.

She looked around and found that she was no longer in her bed; instead, she was standing in a clearing. Coyote was seated nearby staring at an empty space and crying. She felt a powerful need to help him; he seemed so sad, so vulnerable.

She hopped up to him and looked up into his wet eyes. Then something very strange happened, she felt herself transforming into a female coyote, and in a coyote's voice she said, "Tortoise is the oldest and wisest creature on the Scrubland. If you are ever in trouble; ever need advice; go to him. He will know what to do." then the dream ended and she slipped into a deep and restful sleep.

If Rabbit had been in her usual position outside Coyote's den instead of dreaming in her own bed, she would have heard his moaning stop suddenly and his breathing become gentle, and peaceful.

―
―

Coyote woke the next morning and sat up immediately. He knew what he must do! It was so obvious. How could he have forgotten? He must go and consult

Tortoise. After all, he was the oldest and wisest creature on the Scrubland.

He went about his morning routine with a renewed sense of hope. He even managed to go out into the daylight without thinking even once of his stalker; he was just too excited, too focused to notice the Shadow Creature.

He grabbed some breakfast, and spent some time tidying up his fur; he had stopped his usual meticulous grooming and had become ratty looking since his brother's death. When he felt like he looked presentable again, he trotted off to see Tortoise.

Tortoise was dozing in the shade of his favorite pinion tree when a feeling told him he should wake up. He sensed that he was about to have a visitor; and that that visitor was Coyote. He was not surprised; he'd expected that they'd be meeting soon. He took a deep breath and prepared himself for what he knew would be a difficult conversation.

When Coyote entered the circle of his vision, Tortoise instinctively pulled his legs and head into his shell. The in-born survival patterns established across numberless generations were not easy to set aside.

Although Coyote knew he was not the first of his kind to come to Tortoise for counsel, it was the first time that he had sought Tortoise's help. He approached and stood there silently staring at Tortoise. He wasn't sure how this worked. What was he supposed to say?

It was rare for a coyote to have a conversation with any other sort of creature. All other creatures were likely prey for them. As a consequence, few were willing to stand still long enough to strike up an acquaintance; so coyotes mostly limited their social interactions to other coyotes. This coyote had lived alone for so long he was even out of practice in that limited arena.

It was obvious from the way Coyote fidgeted and looked around nervously that he had something on his mind. It was also obvious that he didn't know how to begin. After a few seconds, Tortoise decided to save the old fellow any further discomfort. He extended his head from his shell and, smiling, he looked up at Coyote and said "Good to see you Coyote. Why don't you settle down here in the shade and tell me why you stopped by?"

Coyote looked a bit startled at first; he hadn't expected such a warm welcome. Then, giving Tortoise a shy smile of gratitude and mumbling "Thank you", he settled down and tried to collect his thoughts.

Tortoise waited a few seconds; then he said, "You know, I believe this is the first time in all these years that you and I have talked. I knew your mother well. She was a fine creature and loved her little ones to distraction. She came to me many times to talk about the challenges of raising one or another brood of lively young pups. You were a particular favorite of hers.

She used to tell me what a fine young coyote you were turning out to be." At that, Coyote sighed and let his muzzle rest on his paws. He got a faraway look in his eyes; then he began to speak.

After a slow start, the words tumbled out like a flashflood in an arroyo when rains fall in the foothills. He talked and talked, all about his weak eyes, his white muzzle, his stiff joints, and the run of bad luck he'd been having lately. He even talked about his sadness at losing another chance at a mate and his humiliation at being tricked by the false raven. Then his words seemed to falter and he became silent.

Tortoise could smell the pent up fear hanging unspoken between them. He looked at Coyote and said, "I was sorry to hear about your brother." The truth was out! There was no longer any pretense. It was clear they both knew why Coyote had come; so, he took a deep breath and told the tale of hunting the shadow creature, his brother's strange madness, and his death.

At the end of his story he looked around, fear clear in every movement, and said "Now I've seen it. I've seen the shadow creature! I don't know what to think. Was my brother really crazy? Did I catch the madness from him? Or was he right? Was he being hunted by some terrible foe and am I going to be its next victim?"

Tortoise looked him in the eyes and, in his most reassuring voice, he said, "I can understand how uncomfortable this strange, and unfamiliar situation must make you feel. I remember the first time I noticed the Shadow. It was several years ago. I was confused and frightened until I received an explanation from a much older, wiser friend. She helped me to understand that what I was seeing was not an enemy, nor was it hunting me. It was merely waiting for me. It had, in fact been waiting for me all my life."

"What you are seeing Coyote is your oldest companion. What you call the "Shadow Creature" is not a creature at all, it is your death."

At these words Coyote's eyes grew wide and, even with his old ears, Tortoise could hear his heart pounding. "Death?" he said. "What do you mean Tortoise? Why am I seeing it now?"

Tortoise kept his voice calm and even as he explained. "You see it now because you are old. My own death has been my visible companion for many years. But it did not suddenly arrive at the rising of some fateful dawn; and neither did yours. It has been there all along. You just didn't notice it".

"Each of us has his own death, it is always with us. It is there as we are born. It is watching as we break the shell, or find our mother's breast that first time, and it is there as we grow and master life."

"When we are young, our lives are so full of other distractions we don't notice it lingering there just on the edge of sight. We don't think of it. Instead, we spend our lives ignoring its existence."

"With each new skill we master; each new insight life offers; we assure ourselves that we are not the mortal creatures we are. We want to believe our time is endless and we are unique. But we are not unique and we are not immortal."

"We are Life's creatures, its temporary forms. It is only the Life in us that is constant and the moment must come when we sink back into Life and offer up our substance to craft new forms".

"Our death knows this truth. It waits patiently, reminding us that our time is finite and that each moment, each breath is a precious gift to be cherished and lived consciously".

At first, as he listened to Tortoise, Coyote felt like he was in the middle of a strange dream. The words he was hearing seemed to be about some other creature. He wondered why Tortoise was telling him this. When he realized that the old healer was talking about him; that his own death was the subject of the monolog, panic began to set in.

Coyote could feel his heart beating harder and faster. He knew he should be paying more careful attention to what the quiet, calm voice was saying, but he could not. The sound of his own heartbeat pounding in his ears had reduced Tortoise's words to a soft buzzing. Coyote's heart seemed to be pounding out a message and that message said, "you are going to die"!

He began to feel trapped; to panic; and, in his panic, he felt a growing urge to run, as if, by running away from those terrible words, he could run away from the truth of them.

He began to fidget and look around nervously, as if he were trying to find a way to escape. Suddenly, he stood up and blurted out a thank you; then he turned and raced off into the brush as though he were running for his life.

Rabbit had followed Coyote when he left his den to visit Tortoise. She had stayed hidden, but close enough to hear what they said. When Coyote suddenly stood up and ran off she waited a minute and then hopped over to talk to her mentor.

She was anxious to understand what had happened and what she should do next.

As she drew closer she could see Tortoise gazing into the distance and shaking his head. When he sensed her presence he turned to her and said "Good! I was hoping you were nearby. We need to talk about what is coming and what you must do."

Coyote was running when he left the old healer and he kept running. He didn't have any particular place where he was going. He just wanted to be away from Tortoise and his words; running was all he could think to do, so he ran.

As he ran he kept repeating Tortoise's words over and over to himself "the shadow creature is not a creature at all; it is your death". Each time he came to the phrase "it is your death" he felt a new rush of fear, a new wave of adrenaline pulsed through his system, and he ran.

He ran through the scrublands ignoring all the other creatures in his path. Each small being who saw him racing toward them felt their heart stop for a second; and when he raced past them as though they were invisible, they breathed a sigh of bewildered relief; then sat back and gazed after him wondering, "What has gotten into that crazy old coyote now?"

He ran back and forth across his hunting grounds through the late morning and into the autumn afternoon; until sometime near sunset, he finally couldn't run any more; then he stopped and looked around. "What have you been doing?" he asked himself. And his inner voice said "No Coyote! The question is what are you going to do?"

He realized that he needed to calm down and to think. There must be some way out of this! He was Coyote after all; the Trickster! He could find a way out of any situation if he just thought for a bit. The idea calmed him and he decided to go back to his den and get some rest. In the morning he would head to his spot by the juniper pool and come up with a plan.

Sigman Shapiro

18

When Coyote finally settled down by the juniper pool the first idea that came to him was a simple one. If he was dying, he reasoned, he must be sick. He would go back to see Tortoise and ask him to prescribe some herbal remedy, some course of treatment that would cure this illness. But, when he visited Tortoise the next day, the old healer was not helpful. He looked at Coyote and solemnly shook his head saying "No Coyote. Herbs will not help you. You are not ill. There is no cure for this. You are just old and coming to the end of your time", then he sent him on his way.

Coyote was angry about Tortoise's response. It was obvious that the old healer was not going to help him. For the next few days, he sat by the juniper pool in between hunting trips and mumbled to himself about the ways in which he could get his revenge. After a while, though, he decided that this was not a good way to use his time. He needed to focus on solving the problem.

He had heard that these old healers often presented cleverly disguised riddles to the creatures that came to them; as a way to trick them into finding the answers to their questions themselves. Well, if that was what the old fellow was doing, he was in for a surprise. Coyote was the master of trickery. He would show Tortoise that he had a trick or two of his own!

Tortoise had a serious talk with Rabbit after his first meeting with Coyote. He told her that Coyote was spiraling toward a personal crisis; and that, no matter how painful, disturbing or senseless his actions might seem to her in the weeks ahead, she must limit herself to observing him and restrain her urge to intervene or to feel responsible. He explained the pattern Coyote's actions would follow now that he had been confronted with the truth of his mortality. It was, Tortoise said, important that she let the process take its natural course.

"Then, why am I watching him?" she had asked. "What is the point?"

Tortoise nodded and said, "You must limit yourself to observing him because you will be watching for the critical moment; the moment when all the tricks, and stories, and false ideas he has wrapped himself in all his life have failed him; the moment when he is teetering on the edge. When that moment comes, you must confront him with a choice. The choice he makes will determine the course of the rest of his days."

"You must offer Coyote the path to peace. This is the challenge you were chosen for Rabbit. Above all, you must remember that the choice is his; you can not make it for him and you are not responsible for what he decides."

Shadow Season

THE TORTOISE

Rabbit looked at him and asked, "How will I know when to act and what to do?"

Tortoise spoke to her in his kindest, gentlest voice. "Do not be frightened by this task Rabbit. You are ready for the challenge. You have been preparing for it all your life. I will explain how you will know when the moment is right, and what you must do when it is.

"There is one more thing", Tortoise said. "I expect this process will take much of the coming winter to unfold. That means that I will be in my long sleep when the moment of crisis comes; however you will not be alone. Your spirit guides will be near you. You can call on them whenever you feel the need."

Coyote's next plan was to hide from the shadow. He was certain the shadow could not harm him if it could not find him. He had noticed that he never saw it at night when he was in his own den. He decided that it must spend the night somewhere else, then arrive outside his den in the early morning and follow him from there.

He remembered an abandoned badger's den close to the waterhole; it was one that he was sure the shadow didn't know about. He decided he would sneak off in the middle of the night and hide in this new den. He was certain that he would be safe there; that his death would not know where to find him.

The next day, while he was hunting, he pretended to be following a scent and purposely stepped up to the entrance to the den and checked to see if anyone had moved in. He knew the shadow was watching, so he was careful not to show any sign of his excitement when he saw that it was still unoccupied.

Later that day, as the sun set, he curled up in his old den and pretended to be asleep. Once he was certain that it was completely dark, he slipped quietly out into the night and trotted to the abandoned den.

He worked through the night cleaning out all traces of the former inhabitant and making the space suitable for a coyote. Finally, just before dawn, he settled down and slept.

It was after midday when he woke with a start. At first he was confused. He forgot where he was and how he had got there; then he remembered his plan and he smiled to himself. For the first time in weeks he would be able to step out into the daylight without finding his nemesis waiting. He stood up and sighed with pleasure as he stretched his back; then he trotted out into the sunlight with a big grin on his face.

At first his eyes were dazzled by the afternoon light; then, as he looked around, he saw it, there on the left. It was the shadow! It had found him! Not only was it there waiting for him, but it no longer flitted on the edge of sight. Instead, it was right there where he could see it clearly; a kind of dark, transparent patch that didn't so much block his sight as dim the colors and shapes behind it.

He could feel his initial shock being replaced by anger. How did that thing find him? He turned toward it and growled and bristled. He barked and snapped threats, but the shadow did not move. No matter how fierce he might act it was not frightened by him. It would not be run off that easily!

Since she and Tortoise had spoken, Rabbit had been watching Coyote even more than before. She quickly realized that Tortoise had been right; Coyote's actions had fallen into the pattern Tortoise had described.

He would do a little hunting in the morning; but he would always stop in the early afternoon, whether he was successful or not, and head for his spot by the tiny pool. He would lie there for hours staring into the distance, seeming to do nothing. This might go on for several days, then, suddenly, he would become excited and full of activity. That was the sign that he had come up with another of his "plans".

He seemed to be energized, even happy when set about putting one of his plans into motion. He would become very single minded; his actions focused and deliberate. All of this activity would inevitably lead to the critical moment; the moment when he realized that his plan had failed.

When his plans failed, he would spend the next several days in random fits of angry mumbling and growling until he seemed to run out of energy; then he would sink back into another long spell of lying by the juniper pool and staring into space.

It was a good thing that she had spent months learning about Coyote and watching him struggle with growing old. It helped her understand his actions and feel some sense of compassion for him now that he was approaching this crisis.

—
—

Coyote's initial failures to solve his "problem" did not stop him. He was a hunter, and a hunter's greatest strengths were his tenacity and his ability to focus. He would not be easily discouraged; not when his quarry was his own survival!

Coyote kept up his campaign all through the first half of winter. He was determined to find a way to prove that Tortoise was wrong; that his death was not inevitable.

His supply of ideas seemed to be endless. At one point he decided that fitness was the answer, and he began to run up to the top of the mesa and back every morning before heading out to hunt. He used the regular trail; no more shortcuts for him!

Another time he decided that he had some sort of "poison" in his system and that was why the shadow was following him. For two weeks he took the time to trot across the scrublands to the river every day. There he would immerse himself in the hot, sulfur infused water that flowed from a spring into the river's icy waters.

Although he certainly felt better after weeks of the exercise regimen and the spa treatments, neither of those ideas proved to be a solution, nor, for that matter did any of the dozen or so other ideas he tried.

No matter what he did, everywhere he looked he saw the shadow. In fact, the more he struggled to banish it, the more it seemed to swell up until it threatened to fill all the space in his world.

Eventually his confidence, that, till now, had supported him throughout this ordeal, began to fade. The periods he spent lying by the juniper pool and staring at nothing grew longer and longer. He was losing his will to fight. Gradually his food lost all its taste, the color drained out of his sunsets and the hope drained out of his sunrises.

—

Rabbit poked her nose out of her burrow into the light of another morning in late winter. The sky was clear and the sun was shining but she knew it did not hold much promise of warmth. Still, it felt good on her face, so she hopped out, found a sunny patch of ground and thought about the day ahead.

It would be another day spent checking on Coyote. Rabbit had never been far from him these past weeks.

She had watched his struggles and marveled at his spirit and his cleverness.

Coyote's actions had sometimes seemed strange or even nonsensical to her, but she followed Tortoise's instructions and restrained her urge to intervene. Instead, she had watched him closely looking for the signs Tortoise had described.

She was convinced that now, with spring so close, the critical moment was approaching fast. She had spent the last few weeks preparing the things she would need to play her part.

After warming herself a bit and tidying up her fur, she headed off to check in on Coyote. If her suspicions were right, she would need to act soon.

Her first stop was at the juniper pool. Coyote's morning hunting runs had dwindled down in frequency a while ago until, most mornings, he went straight to the clearing in the juniper grove and spent his entire day there. Recently he had even stopped leaving his den to lie by the pool.

As she suspected, he was not there. So, she headed to his den to see if he was holed up there like he had been for the past week or more.

When she arrived outside his den she hopped as close to the entrance as she dared and paused to sniff the air and to listen. What she heard was the sound of Coyote's slow, quiet breathing from inside the den. He was preparing to spend another day withdrawn and immobile. This was clearly the sign that Tortoise had told her about.

The time had come for her to act.

When he thought about it later, Coyote realized that he had known all along that Tortoise held the answer to his problem. His mistake was, believing that Tortoise had to tell him what was required. What he finally understood was, Tortoise was living the answer.

Everyone knew that Tortoise was by far the oldest creature in the scrublands. He had already been ancient when Coyote was a pup. When Coyote thought about this, he realized that Tortoise must have some secret that helped him live longer than all the other creatures around him. Coyote was not sure what that secret was, but he was pretty sure that, if he thought about it hard enough he could figure it out.

With that thought in mind, he spent the next several days recalling everything he knew or had been told about Tortoise and the way he lived. In the end he had come to three ideas that he considered significant.

First, the old healer almost never went anywhere. He could almost always be found resting quietly in the pinion grove near his burrow. Second, he never ate anything but moist, juicy plants. The green pads of wild prickly pears were his favorite food. Third, was

Tortoise's long sleep. Every winter he crawled into his burrow and slept until spring.

Coyote reasoned that the combination of these three factors was the secret to Tortoise's longevity and that he would gain the same benefits if he adopted the same behavior.

His first task was to gather a supply of juicy green food. He headed over to a big patch of prickly pear cactus that grew near his den. Normally he avoided the sharp spines of the cactus at all cost. Even his thick winter coat could not offer much protection against the painful spines.

When he arrived he sat down and studied the problem. After a few failed attempts he limped off back home to pull the spines from his paws and his muzzle and think about what to do. The next day he arrived back at the cactus patch pushing a large, round rock ahead of him with his nose. He rolled the rock over a cactus pad and, just as he had hoped, it broke off the spines. Unfortunately, it also ground the pad into a sandy pulp. He trotted off and returned a while later pushing a slightly smaller rock. This one did the trick. When he nosed it over a cactus pad, it broke off the spines and left the pad intact. He had found the answer.

He spent the next few days cleaning the spines off cactus and carrying the disarmed pads down into his den. The process was not perfect, when he finished he had quite a few painful wounds on his muzzle and paws; but he also had a good supply of juicy cactus pads in his den.

When his stockpile seemed large enough, he trotted into his den and settled down. Spring was not far off and he was determined to stay there and sleep until it arrived. If he got hungry or thirsty the juicy cactus would provide the food and liquid he needed.

Once Rabbit was satisfied that the right moment had come, she went back to her burrow and prepared. When everything was ready, she settled down and cleared her mind. She was waiting for dark to be sure that Coyote was sleeping when she started.

After a while she sensed that the time was right and she began meditating like Tortoise had taught her.

Gradually, she lost her sense of time passing. Her surroundings seemed to grow dim and almost transparent. She found herself standing in her burrow looking at a small female rabbit who seemed to be asleep.

She nodded and then turned to walk out the entrance into bright sunlight. She had left her world behind and entered a new place; one that was both unknown and, at the same time, strangely familiar.

Once outside, she found herself standing on a trail in a narrow valley. She was surrounded by lush vegetation.

Everything was bathed in soft, warm light. She felt peaceful.

She looked around and smiled; then she remembered that she was waiting for someone. She nodded and hopped into the bushes by the trail. She had just settled down to wait when she heard the sound of someone coming. When she looked up, she saw an old coyote with a blissful smile coming down the trail toward her.

Coyote had been holed up in his den for several days. It had not been a pleasant experience. He was bored and restless lying in the dim light hour after hour. Also, it hadn't taken him long to realize that cactus pads were miserable food for a coyote. They tasted awful and they upset his stomach terribly. The worst thing of all was, no matter how many he forced himself to eat, they could not satisfy his hunger.

At first he had to fight the urge to bolt from the den and find some proper food – even some carrion would be preferable to this nasty green stuff. But, then he would remember the shadow and he would get control of himself.

He comforted himself with the thought of his triumph. He couldn't wait to see Tortoise's reaction when he learned that Coyote had found the old healer's secret to avoiding death.

After a few days he was beginning to grow weak from lack of proper nourishment. All he could do was doze and dream. A few times he thought he saw the shadow sitting in the corner watching him. He told himself it was only a dream and then he slipped back into his fitful sleep.

At last, when his energy was almost gone, he fell into a deep, peaceful sleep.

Coyote found himself standing on a trail in a deep, narrow valley. The trail was bathed in gentle sunlight and surrounded by dense, lush vegetation. He could see that it stretched for a short distance ahead, then turned a corner around a mesquite tree and disappeared into the undergrowth.

It was not a trail he recognized, but he had a strong sense that he should go forward down the path to see where it led. When he reached the tree, he turned to look back. The path behind him was no longer there! There was only a kind of thick mist. For some reason he seemed to expect this. He turned back to the trail and continued down the valley.

As he trotted along he could hear the singing of birds and the buzzing of insects. All around him the plants were in bloom and their scents filled the air. Dozens of small creatures, lizards, voles, snakes, rabbits, every kind of creature that lived in the scrublands, were moving through the brush, going about their everyday lives.

He was filled with a sense of peace and he felt that everything was "right". He realized that he was happy; and that he hadn't been happy in a long time. That was when the rabbit appeared out of the brush and fell in hopping beside him.

This too seemed right. It was as though he had been waiting for her. She looked up at him and smiled. Then he heard her say "Come with me Coyote. I have something to show you. It's just a little further down this trail." He nodded and smiled at her as they continued on.

He wasn't sure how long they traveled together; his sense of time seemed distorted; but, eventually they came out of the valley and were standing on a high rock outcropping above a wide clearing with three trails that led out the other side.

From where he stood, Coyote could see that the left-hand trail was muddy, shrouded in gloom, and rain fell on it without let up. The right-hand trail was exposed to blazing sunlight and lined with sharp rocks and cactus.

The middle trail was very different; it seemed to be a continuation of the one he had just left. Like that one, it plunged down into a narrow valley filled with vegetation and teeming with life.

He turned to his companion and started to ask her what this was about; but she held up a paw to silence him and pointed off into the distance. He followed her gesture with his eyes and saw that the valley that was the route of the middle trail seemed to fade in the distance and was swallowed up in a deep, dark shadow. He stared at it for a second and then the thought came to him that this was the shadow that had haunted him for months; the shadow that Tortoise had said was his death.

He felt a shiver run down his spine and he turned again to the rabbit to ask her what was happening. Again she held up her paw for silence and then she pointed down into the clearing.

Coyote looked down where she was pointing and there he saw a coyote; one that he hadn't noticed before. The coyote was old; the tips of his ears and tail were gray and the fur of his muzzle was snowy white. He was turning and turning restlessly, as though he could not decide which trail to take. He would take a step toward the right-hand trail and then he would pull back and turn to the middle trail. He would take a step toward that trail and then he would pull back and turn to the left-hand trail. He repeated these motions over and over without committing himself to any path.

Coyote turned to the rabbit and asked her "Why is he spinning like that? Why doesn't he just pick one?"

Rabbit looked at him and said, "Which one would you pick?"

Coyote looked at the middle trail and smiled; but, then his eyes traveled along its path until he came to the shadow that was clearly at its end. When he saw where it ended he shivered and shook his head. "I'd take the right trail, he said. "I grew up in the scrublands and I am comfortable with the sun and cactus."

No sooner had he said those words than the coyote below stopped spinning; he turned to the right and raced down the sunny trail. The coyote had only gone a short distance when he began to stumble from the heat and fall into the rocks and scratch himself on the cactus spines. As he continued down the trail his struggles increased and he started to snarl and snap as though he were under attack. After a while the trail bent to the right and the coyote was out of sight; even then Coyote could hear him cursing, yelping in pain, growling, and threatening his unseen adversaries.

In a few minutes, the old coyote reappeared on the edge of the clearing looking tired and tattered. The right-hand trail seemed to be a circle. It had brought him right back to where he had started.

When he stepped back out into the clearing, the whole scene seemed to lurch and, though he wasn't sure, Coyote thought he saw the shadow at the end of the middle trail move a short distance closer.

The rabbit looked at him again and said, "Now which trail would you pick?"

Coyote looked at the choices again. Again he was drawn to the middle trail; and again, when he saw the shadow at its end he shook his head and said "I would take the cooler trail on the left."

As soon as he said the words, the coyote below turned to the left and raced into the rain. He had only gone a short distance when he became mired in mud and soaked to the skin. He worked hard to pull himself forward, but it was clear that every step was a struggle. Soon his tail was dragging and his muzzle was drooping. Even his ears seemed to sag. After a while the trail turned to the left and Coyote could no longer see him, but he could hear him weeping and bewailing his fate as he slogged down the trail.

In a few minutes it became clear to Coyote that the left-hand trail, like the one on the right, was a circle. The old coyote reappeared on the left edge of the clearing coated in mud and looking exhausted. As he stepped back into the clearing the whole scene lurched once again. This time Coyote was watching and he definitely saw the shadow move a short distance closer.

Coyote looked at the rabbit and waited for her to ask him the question. Instead, she pointed to the old coyote below. He was no longer spinning from trail to trail; instead he leaped toward the right-hand trail. The result was the same as before. The coyote fought his way down the trail being battered and wounded by his own struggles and then he reappeared at the clearing limping and looking even more exhausted than before.

Shadow Season

THE THREE PATHS

Once again when he stepped into the clearing the shadow moved up the middle valley toward him.

The old coyote didn't hesitate this time either, he trotted straight over to the left-hand trail and crawled off to weep and struggle through the mud again.

Coyote spoke out loud, half to himself, "Why would he keep taking those trails when he knows it is pointless and it makes him miserable?" The rabbit did not respond.

Now things began to speed up. Coyote watched in horror as the creature below moved from the right trail to the left trail and back to the right with greater and greater speed. Each time he returned to the clearing he looked sadder and more bedraggled. And each time the shadow drew closer to him.

The rabbit looked at him as if she were waiting for him to say something. Coyote wanted to shout "Stop", but his voice would not work. Finally, he summoned all his strength and began to shout. Then the scene went black.

He could feel himself falling through the blackness, and, as he fell, he could hear the rabbit saying "You can not avoid death. You can only choose how you spend the days until death comes. How many more days will you waste?"

Coyote woke with his heart pounding. Something was puzzling him. It seemed to have something to do with a strange phrase that was repeating in his mind "How many more days will you waste?"

Every time he thought of those words he felt weary and sad, as though he was bearing a terrible burden; one that he had been carrying for a long time and hadn't noticed before.

He sat in his den until his heart calmed down; then he felt a strong urge to go outside and feel the sun on his face again. He rose onto his shaky legs and trotted slowly past the pile of cactus pads to the entrance to his den.

As he approached the opening, he could smell a wonderful aroma. It was the sweet scent of life; the scent of his home, and it was drawing him outside. He stepped into the soft, warm light of the scrublands morning and his heart filled with joy. He could feel how much he loved this place and all the life in it. It was something he hadn't felt in a long time. It seemed to him that when he was younger it had been with him all the time. It felt so right, so good, he couldn't help but wonder why he had ever let go of it.

Then he remembered the words that had been in his head when he woke "How many more days will you waste?" He wasn't sure what it meant, but he was sure that the answer was important. He needed to grab something nutritious to eat and then he would go off to the juniper pool and sit and think about it.

As he headed off down the trail to hunt up a meal he glanced to the left and noticed a sort of shadow flickering on the edge of sight. It seemed familiar so he smiled and nodded to it and it seemed to nod back at him.

He turned as if to continue down the trail, but paused looking perplexed; there was something he was going to think about. What was it? It seemed to have slipped his mind. He looked around as if the answer were somewhere in the warm spring air, the scented sage blossoms, the songs of the birds, or the busy hum of the insects.

"Ah well", he thought. "It'll come to me later. This is far too beautiful a morning to waste sitting around thinking". And he set off down the trail with a light step and an even lighter heart.

Epilogue

It was several years later and Rabbit was sitting in the shade of Tortoise's pinion tree. She was no longer the young rabbit who had helped Coyote confront the Shadow. In fact she had become a matronly rabbit known throughout this part of the scrublands as a wise and compassionate counselor.

Coyote had long ago made the Great Transformation and even Tortoise had stepped into the shadows.

She had just finished listening to a burrowing owl talk about her son who was at the age to go out on his own and start a family, but he was refusing to leave the family burrow. She had paid careful attention to the story and agreed that she would speak to the youngster tomorrow and see if she could help ease him through this confusing and frightening time, it was the sort of thing she was known for, her specialty.

All the while she had been listening to the distressed owl she had kept one eye on a very young tortoise who was lingering on the fringes of their conversation, trying to be as inconspicuous as possible. He had been hanging around nearby observing her every day for the last several weeks but had not spoken to her.

She had tried to speak to him a few times, but he always pulled into his shell and pretended to be sleeping. In a way, he reminded her of herself when she was young, lingering near Tortoise; irresistibly drawn to learn from him and too shy to ask.

She was just about to try one more time, when a dozen or so young rabbits came hopping up giggling and chattering. She smiled and said "so little ones, what can I do for you today?"

"Please Old Mother" the boldest one said, "Please tell us a story."

She nodded and said, "Of course. Everyone settle down and I'll begin". She glanced at the young tortoise and saw that he was inching his way closer to the group.

The young rabbits arranged themselves around her and became very quiet. When she could see that the tortoise had settled in on the right edge of the group she began, "Today I am going to tell you a tale about a coyote; a rabbit, and a difficult journey they made together, and how a very wise tortoise helped them find their way."

THE WEB

About the Author

Sigman Shapiro is a native Californio and a recent transplant to the beautiful state of Colorado. He is an avid reader, hiker, poet, cook, gardener, friend of trees, and lover of life. His poetry can be found at www.infloressence.wordpress.com. He can be contacted at dishes78154@mypacks.net

About the Illustrator

Brenda Erickson resides in New Jersey with her supportive spouse. Her art originates in the space where dreams begin; combining nature, fantasy and joy. Her goal in her artistic expression is to honor the divine in the world around her and within herself. She can be reached via her portfolio website at vividmusings.com.